Finding Light in the Darkness

How businesses, organisations and teams adapted to the pandemic, and the lessons for other challenges and crises.

Jon Key

Copyright © 2024 by Jon Key.

All rights reserved. No part of this book may be reproduced or used in any manner without written permission of the copyright owner except for the use of quotations in a book review. For more information, email: corporate@keyand.co.

www.keyandco.org.

Contents

Introduction	3
1. Putting It All To The Test	11
2. A Crisis, But Seeing The Funny Side	23
3. Rowing The Void	33
4. Banking On The Team	45
5. The Beacon Of Hope	53
6. Always A Reason To Celebrate	61
7. Keeping Mentally Moored While At Sea	71
8. Late Night Lessons Of Key And Co.	81
9. The Angel's Share from the Devil's Cut	89
10. Keeping on Running	101
11. Out of our Depth: An Endurance Swimmer's Lessons	111
12. A New Chapter And Long COVID	123
Weaving The Common Threads	135
Reflections Three Years On	141
Lessons For Future Crises	151

Timeline	155
Acknowledgments	157
About the Author	159
Getting in Touch	161

To all those who find light in the darkness.

Introduction

There is a saying: the best indicator of future behaviour is past behaviour. In that light, I believe reflection is essential for anyone who is looking to move forward in a new capacity. Are you learning from the past? Or are you doomed to repeat it? We all have a lot to reflect on from the recent COVID-19 global pandemic. From team members to leaders of organisations, from social clubs to businesses, from front-line activists to at-home observers – no matter where you find yourself on the spectrum, I have gathered stories and insights in this book to help you reflect on your own experiences during the pandemic. The case studies are intended to trigger your own thoughts on what you learned from the pandemic and how you will apply this to the future. I hope you find the book both interesting and thought-provoking. I invite you to take the lessons from these pages as we all move on from the pandemic and face future challenges, from the day-to-day local challenges to fundamental global ones.

This isn't to say there is another pandemic on the way that I want to prepare the world for, although it could happen. Rather, I want to showcase the value of applying the pandemic lessons laterally to other challenges you might be facing today or in the future. From running a successful team through the daily task list to tackling your business's challenges to finding solutions for other existential threats.

Before COVID-19 struck, Key & Co., my consulting network, worked with businesses large and small, public and private, to overcome their most pressing issues. We were also the "flies on the wall" as we observed how CEOs and leadership teams came to terms with the pandemic crisis. We offered insight as they weighed their options to make the difficult but necessary decisions to navigate an extraordinary three years.

The pandemic was a truly, global disaster. As of 28th December 2022, according to the World Health Organisation (WHO), there had been 650 million confirmed cases and nearly 7 million deaths from COVID-19. The figures suggest significant under-reporting, and nobody knows the actual numbers. Of the confirmed cases, 269 million were in Europe, 185 million were in The Americas, 104 million were in Western Pacific, 61 million were in South-East Asia, 23 million were in Eastern Mediterranean, and 9 million were in Africa. North Korea reported zero deaths or cases. We may never know the true human cost, but a Cambridge University report estimated the global economy could be impacted by as much as $82 trillion.

At Key & Co., our privileged position and close relationships with our clients during this time allowed us to observe how businesses and organisations adapted to survive the pandemic and emerged in a stronger position, including: effective leadership, purpose, innovation, agility, teamwork, decision-making, customer relationships, planning, and resilience. These lessons were the subject of my previous book, *Late Night Lessons From The COVID-19 Crisis*.

The clients in our network include global logistics businesses that distributed goods and supplies worldwide and technology companies that kept us all connected. We watched as our global commodity clients distributed essential resources and banks provided cash and financial services. We even supported national health services that treated the sick, retailers who sold crucial groceries, and utilities that kept the heat running and the water flowing.

While we are proud of our portfolio of large, international clients, we also advised small businesses and sole traders who looked to us for guidance as they navigated the crisis. It was those smaller businesses and organisations where the lessons seemed to be most pertinent, for these businesses were pushed closest to the brink and were therefore the ones that had to dig deepest to survive. Remaining positive through the period was a huge challenge for small business owners. A survey of these carried out during the pandemic in Australia revealed one in 5 suffered mental health issues. Staying positive was particularly important for this group.

For my network and our clients, the COVID-19 crisis was a period of extraordinary challenges. Could they survive a sudden decimation of their revenue? How would they continue to make a living or keep their doors open? What tactics and strategies were available to keep their ships afloat?

In this short volume, you will find twelve case studies that highlight the lessons of agility and survival of people and businesses who faced their greatest challenge: confronting a global pandemic. The list is deliberately eclectic, wide-ranging, and includes:

1. The medical company, reinventing itself as a COVID-19 testing business, growing from 0 to more than 2,000 employees and contractors in two years while supplying millions of tests to keep businesses and households safe through the lockdown;

2. The stand-up comedian reliant on live venues who pivoted

to writing books and hosting Zoom gigs. Ultimately reaching a global audience from Argentina to Zambia and helping businesses learn valuable lessons of positivity and resilience from comedy;

3. The elite rowing squad that was forced to train in isolation. Focused on a single race that was off, then on, then off, then on again. Staying positive and ultimately winning the race while also keeping up with their studies. Through it all, finding innovative approaches to training that have carried through to post-lockdown;

4. The European bank that survived the pandemic shock and thrived while building new products and fostering a culture of collaboration, all while transforming the business and returning the bank to profit;

5. A church, with its congregation in lockdown, becoming a beacon of hope with Zoom services and home deliveries. The vicar grows the congregation during the lockdown while officiating at funerals and weddings and staying positive through the dark times;

6. The baking business "dependent" on the in-person parties, weddings, and events that were vanquished by the pandemic. Now, pivoting to reinvent its home delivery service and establish the world's #1 online premium cake-making training course to inspire others to follow suit;

7. The chaplains who worked tirelessly to support the seafarers who kept the world moving. These seafarers were in a tough situation; separated from their families, unable to go ashore

or get home all while transporting essential goods during the lockdown and looking for their light in the darkness;

8. The business consultant, trapped in his home office, without the ability to work closely with clients and colleagues. Still, he managed to achieve record results by supporting clients through the lockdown with strategic and financial advice, coaching, and leadership motivation;

9. A sustainable whisky distillery that weathered the crisis, keeping the team safe, and building a new and novel brand that takes the market by storm, transforming the whisky industry forever;

10. An athletics club that kept training through the pandemic, its members keeping safe and staying physically and mentally fit, smashing personal bests while adapting to the situation.

11. The endurance swimmer, drawing on her inner strength to navigate the pandemic, and pivoting her speaking business to an online model, with lessons for us all for another pandemic and other challenges.

12. The rower, whose Olympic dream was thwarted by the pandemic and who is now raising awareness of the long COVID pandemic that continues to affect millions of people.

All twelve stories feature very different situations but share some common threads. Every one of them highlights the importance of a strong purpose and vision when facing tough times. Their survival demonstrates how having a guiding light or "north star" is essential to keep a team moving in the same direction. All highlight the importance of leadership and the importance of culture. Whether it be an elite sports team, a church community, a financial services business, or a healthcare business, the lessons are as clear as they are universal.

Above all, we discovered the most successful businesses and teams all displayed the importance of positivity. They never gave up. They leant into the crisis. They found energy and motivation when they had to.

They found light in the darkness.

In a way, these lessons aren't terribly surprising. But then again, never before have we experienced them at such a large scale in stark observability. And with the experience of COVID-19 fresh in our minds, we have a unique opportunity to reflect on the lessons and to apply them to other challenges and future crises.

In particular, the other obvious existential threat that hangs over all of us is climate change. Not only will every one of us need to be at the top of our game to address this complicated issue, but we will certainly need to draw on what so many of us learnt over the past few years. Many of the lessons from the pandemic can be directly applied to discovering what we need to do to address climate change as individuals, teams, companies, and governments.

"However vast the darkness, we must supply our own light."
— Stanley Kubrik

Chapter One

Putting It All To The Test

A new company, borne out of the pandemic, growing from 0 to over 2,000 employees and contractors in two years while supplying over 5 million tests to keep workplaces, businesses and travellers safe through the lockdown.

The scariest part of the early days of the pandemic was the unknown. We knew there was a highly transmissible respiratory disease that was making thousands of people all over the world extremely sick. We knew it was travelling fast, but we didn't know how it transmitted or how to protect ourselves. We didn't know what to do to fight the virus because we had so little data to help us determine our next step.

Couple this uncertainty with the variance of the disease and how it presents, and COVID-19 proved to be a tricky disease to track. Some people were hospitalised and died from respiratory failure, while others were completely asymptomatic. This wasn't like responding to the annual flu that comes around every year. This time, scientists and policymakers were starved of information. And given the unpredictable nature of the virus, entrepreneurs saw a need to collate and provide vital information to support the global health response.

Fortunately, highly accurate tests for the virus were quickly created. The challenge was building up the laboratory capacity and capability to meet the need created by a pandemic and the safety and well-being assurance of an accurate, sensitive test result. Solving this challenge would enable swift action to isolate and treat those affected. Testing needed to take the express lane; thus, Cignpost Diagnostics was born.

In April 2020, *Project Little Boat* (PLB) launched. It was a not for profit organisation of volunteers and business leaders that came together to try and utilise their experience and know-how in the fight against coronavirus. An early member of PLB was Christian Corney, who had a background in leading fast paced, consumer-focused businesses. Faced with a new challenge, Christian volunteered for PLB as they developed a proof of concept for a rapid, mobile COVID-19 testing protocol. Project Little Boat was aiming to assist the UK's care home sector and proposed their ideas to government. The UK government received PLB's ideas warmly, but its strategy wasn't deployed. Despite the attractiveness, the government's preference was for larger nationwide project management solutions, rightly appropriate for such a global health challenge. It was perhaps unsurprising then that the bureaucrats and entrepreneurs did not come together. However, whilst the government could not commit to PLB, it was clear that others could benefit from their ideas and initiatives. As such, Cignpost

Diagnostics was born. A business created to develop these concepts and offer them to organisations that were desperate for solutions that would help them get back to what they do best.

One organisation, in particular, was raring to get back into action – The Professional Golf Association European Tour. As golf is already a sport of social distancing, a few players on several hundred acres of fairway, the association was ready to get tournaments back underway and players back on tour. At the time, global sports franchises were exploring ways of returning to at least some sense of normality. They were looking to identify partners who might be able to create bio-security strategies to bring back the competition. Cignpost Diagnostics thus began working with the PGA. With a client on the books, Cignpost Diagnostics founders asked Christian to lead the new venture and the first mobile laboratory was rolled out on to the golf course.

The first tests were administered to high-profile sporting and entertainment personalities. The proof of concept was a huge success, enabling a televised small-scale event to go ahead. The film crews present immediately saw the benefit of the operating model; safe, secure working environments facilitated by on-location laboratories and clinical operations. It was a one-stop shop, point-of-care solution that enabled rapid COVID-19 testing. This was a huge departure from the traditional laboratory approach, which didn't come close to what modern, entertainment clients needed. From that moment, Cignpost Diagnostics experienced explosive growth. Not only did they successfully set up testing facilities and "safe bubble" protocols for the golf tournament, but they were quickly signed on to provide similar environments for other professional competitions. Over time Christian and his team facilitated testing sites in 21 countries for 83 tournaments – administering 50,000 tests overall – bringing back the spirit of competition to golf. Cignpost's professionalism and high standards quickly saw them in high demand, and over time they would provide testing for some of the world's highest profile elite sports franchises and events in athletics, golf, football, rugby, tennis, motorsports and more.

As for the camera crews and producers who watched how Cignpost set up the safe bubbles for the first golf tournament? They wanted it too. Media producers – like TV and movie studios – were already looking for ways to get their crews back to work and producing content again. However, they were restricted by the fact that traditional labs were turning tests around in days. Cignpost was returning test results in hours. Thanks to innovations from Cignpost's scientific leadership, they reduced the benchmark turnaround time for a gold standard PCR test from six hours to two. Furthermore, they were developing testing protocols that identified infected people who were not yet *infectious*, so they could remove them before they compromised the safe bubbles – a breakthrough in workplace bio-security. This approach was transformative in the field of media production, and Cignpost quickly became the go-to partner for the world's most prestigious content and media production companies.

Cignpost Diagnostics initially focused on the corporate or B2B market needs for testing, but quickly identified the need to develop a consumer facing brand and ExpressTest was created in anticipation of forthcoming demand. Pandemic restrictions were easing, with some countries reopening international travel. ExpressTest was positioned as the go-to provider for the "Fit To Fly" credentials necessary to travel. Their testing centres were set up in some of the biggest airports – Heathrow, Gatwick, Glasgow and Edinburgh. Quickly their testing sites could be found in high streets and shopping centres across the UK.

PUTTING IT ALL TO THE TEST

The growth of the COVID-19 testing business was swift, but the demand for the tests far outpaced the supply of the equipment needed to administer them. Before COVID there would have been an industry-wide surplus of diagnostic capacity, now there were global shortages across the board. Basic consumables were subject to huge demand, creating global supply chain restrictions of essentials such as latex gloves, masks and other PPE. Also scarce was laboratory equipment such as PCR machines, and even basic consumables like pipettes and swabs. On top of these challenges, Christian knew they mustn't get it wrong. When it came to COVID-19, the trust of the public was paramount. Minor errors would have real, human consequences with potentially catastrophic results. Why take the test if the results couldn't be trusted? Other testing providers were issuing thousands of incorrect test results, potentially resulting in additional deaths and a further spread of COVID-19 amongst the most vulnerable. This was unacceptable.

Bad-apple testing companies took advantage, putting profits before people and eroding trust in an emergent industry that was there to help people when they needed it the most. This wasn't the strategy for Christian. Things would be done the right way. It wasn't just about building a company that tested for COVID-19, but creating a corporate culture centred on purpose. Early on, Cignpost established its mission and defined a set values for the organisation that reinforced and strengthened as the company grew. Internally, the company promoted the pursuit of excellence and principles of trust. They removed fear from decision-making so the company could scale faster and established a collaborative "no blame" culture to enable them to rapidly address failures in the system, empowering people to achieve the highest standards. In turn, the business was rewarded with a highly motivated team, heavily invested in the Cignpost mission. The company codified these values early on and reinforced them often. They won significant contracts to provide COVID-19 testing for elite sports and media franchises by staying true to these values, earning and retaining customer trust.

As well as developing a culture of continuous improvement, Cignpost focused hard on recruiting the right people. Over the first three months, they brought together a team through trusted personal networks, contracting those they knew would be the right cultural fit, working in a complementary way and bought into the mission as the need to expand capability arose. Then as it became clear the business was going to last longer than a short spell, Christian and the team turned their attention to attracting individuals that could enable Cignpost to develop into the organisation it knew it could become. Hiring for "tomorrow", Christian built a leadership team of diverse talent and diverse thought. "We created a business that combined unparalleled scientific expertise with entrepreneurial commercial acumen". In this way, Cignpost was able to bring together operational dynamism, with laboratory and clinical excellence to deliver the highest standards within an industry-disrupting product solution.

Cignpost's focus was on its mission of making people safe. Safe to go about their daily lives, return to work, and get back to the things they love. Safe to visit their loved ones and safe to travel. Providing affordable, accurate and reliable diagnostic services gave people a greater sense of well-being, knowing they could live and work together without fear of infection. Being together was something people had been restricted from and Cignpost helped to bring them together.

The results were remarkable. The company grew from incorporation to employing more than 2,000 people. It delivered over 5 million tests and generating hundreds of millions in revenue - something that would take a decade or more for most other companies. Growing this quickly meant staying resourceful and agile in area of the business, from managing supply chains, adopting strict legislative regulations, building all the necessary business functions from scratch, motivating and leading teams and everything else a company might face over such an accelerated lifespan. Cignpost condensed the growth lifecycle of a business into months rather than years. This huge growth rate had a massive effect on both the business and its people. They were passionate and driven, knowing that they were making a real impact for the better, but the relentlessness of COVID-19 meant they were at risk of burnout. To keep the team together and moving forward, Christian would host town halls every two or three weeks. Sharing progress through stories of achievement helped everyone visualise how the company was making a difference. Internal communications were key in galvanising the ever-expanding workforce to retain, propagate and reinforce its core values and purpose. Culture was critical to the success. In a time when the world seemed isolated, when masks and social distancing had us feeling alone, these gatherings were essential in maintaining a sense of community for everyone within the organisation. Employees and contractors knew that they were a part of something special and would do what they could to deliver – the light they could rely on to navigate the darkness.

Christian and the leadership team worked non-stop to deliver on the demands of a hyper-growth business driven by commitment to the customer. Those who were putting their trust in Cignpost. Those who were waiting on a test result to see if they could work or play, visit a loved one or go on that holiday that they were so longing for. There was always something needing to be done. A huge challenge was establishing a supply chain where global demand outstripped supply. Implementing over 90 labs and clinical sites was a big part of the challenge, as well as keeping up with the complexity of evolving the scientific practices to meet various Government and client demands, whilst also meeting mandatory legislative accreditation in record time. In the beginning, Christian worked round the clock from his attic room to ensure he was on hand to fight fires, make decisions and drive the organisation forwards. The entire team repeatedly displaying resilience and endurance as they exhausted themselves to meet the needs of industry and public alike. But, throughout, Christian felt it was all worthwhile. Amongst the highest accolades he recalls from the time was receiving the mark of excellence from Trustpilot, the UK's foremost customer satisfaction tracker, and especially how the Cignpost staff were so warmly regarded by the customers they served. "Becoming the most trusted provider in the country was a testament to the dedication, commitment and passion shown by an amazing group of people that were single-minded in their pursuit of excellence. Our belief that, unlike other companies, a test result was not just a column in a spreadsheet but a human being with fears and hopes, who was relying on Cignpost to get it right, on time and 100% accurate."

What made these accomplishments possible? In retrospect, some of the essential factors to Cignpost's success were strong leadership and empowered employees working in a values-based culture. Along with its strong, unifying purpose, the company used its agility to innovate and act decisively in response to a highly dynamic and uncertain environment, swiftly responding to both needs and opportunities.

All of this was fascinating for me to observe. Cignpost was a Key & Co. client during the pandemic. During the first lockdown, I took a call from a former colleague who was working there. He was asking for help with their travel-testing business and asking an impossible question: "how long will the pandemic last?" These are just the kind of questions Key & Co. likes to help business to solve and we worked on an intense project to help them to think about various scenarios during the pandemic.

Meanwhile, scientists were working night and day to tackle the pandemic. UK scientists led the way in developing a COVID-19 vaccine. Lead times were slashed as teams worked round the clock to produce the first vaccine in less than a year. By December 2022, 94% of the population over 12, or 53 million people, had received the first dose of the vaccine and the second dose was received by 80%, or 50 million.

All pandemics come to an end eventually, though. Even COVID-19 needed to taper off, which meant an eventual reduction in the demand for testing. When this day inevitably came, where would Cignpost go next? This was something Christian, and the team put a lot of thought into. COVID was the opportunity they needed to scale up the business with a high-demand product. The pandemic proved to be (hopefully) a once-in-a-lifetime opportunity, and they seized on it perfectly. They built a brand and business committed to professional excellence that had earned the trust of millions of customers through delivering a level of service that was the envy of an industry. The belief was that Cignpost could take that core set of values and commitment to customer wellbeing and create a next-generation healthcare proposition that would positively impact people's health and lives. For Cignpost, there are now two questions to answer: what can we make of the next opportunity? And can we be observant enough to see it coming?

Christian knows his long-term future will have more planning compared to the instantaneous, reactive choices that had shaped the years of the pandemic. How can he translate the innovative approach, agility, rapid decision-making, and risk-taking into something the post-pandemic world needs? The need for information about diseases and health conditions is still there, and healthcare companies worldwide are applying COVID-19 lessons to other diagnostic services. Necessity may be the mother of invention, and Christian knows it is only a matter of time before the company shapes its priorities around a new, pertinent need. Everyone involved with Cignpost Diagnostics throughout the pandemic crisis learnt that the extraordinary is possible with the combination of agility, purpose, culture, teamwork and passion.

"MAYBE YOU HAVE TO know the darkness before you can appreciate the light."
— Madeline L'Engle

Chapter Two

A Crisis, But Seeing The Funny Side

Reliant on live shows before the pandemic, a stand-up comedian draws on his resilience and wit to pivot to writing books and performing gigs on Zoom, reaching a global audience from Argentina to Zambia.

"Hello, I'm Stuart Goldsmith. I interview the funniest people in the world and ask them in depth about how they do it and how they cope with the challenges of a creative life. I've spoken with over 400 comics: people like Jimmy Carr, James Acaster, Stewart Lee, Sarah Millican, Sindhu Vee, Bill Burr, and Russell Howard." And so begins another of the more than 400 instalments of The *Comedian's Comedian* podcast – an award-winning production celebrating over 20 million downloads to listeners worldwide since it began in 2012.

With the podcast, Stu's goal is simple: to create something *"for anyone who writes comedy, makes comedy, loves comedy, or just has an interest in comedians and what makes them so annoying."* The podcast was a natural progression for his comedy career, which had spanned the globe and yielded numerous awards, including winning the 2013 New Zealand Comedy Festival's Spirit of the Fridge Award and the Malcolm Hardee Award at the 2012 Edinburgh Comedy Festival. Stu Goldsmith's career began as one half of a comedy act called The Unknown Stuntmen - which won the Scottish Busking Championship in 2001. He went on to perform solo in Covent Garden, where he would walk a tug-of-war tightrope pulled on by ten men, all while eating a packet of crisps. It only went upward and outward from there. Stu has performed numerous times at the Montreal Just For Laughs Festival, the Melbourne International Comedy Festival, and is one of the few UK comics invited to perform at the South by Southwest festival in Austin, Texas. He is also the regular studio warm up comic for the Graham Norton Show on the BBC.

His career as a comic and forensic investigator of his peers led naturally to public speaking to corporate clients about cultivating resilience and solving problems under pressure. As a comic, he has an inherent ability to collaborate, take risks, and maintain mental flexibility in real time while entertaining an audience. Through his podcast, he learned that "the defining characteristic of comics is not that we're funny; it's that we are resilient." Like comics, he says, business leaders are often the most powerful and vulnerable in the room. "When I share my insights on resilience from the world's greatest comics, it helps leaders take responsibility for their own 'bouncebackability.'" These insights have helped businesses from all over the world, including Hg Capital, Deloitte, LEGO, eBay, BBC, Comic Relief, and many more.

Stu has been a speaker at our company events over the past few years. He and I got to know each other just before the pandemic, and he spoke to the team and our clients in 2019 before the lockdown but as the virus was spreading. At the core of Stu's entire career is stand-up comedy. A room, a stage, a microphone, and a crowd of people who want to laugh. He specialises in stand-up, and stand-up relies on the energy of face-to-face, in-person events, often in intimate venues with audiences packed into small spaces. COVID-19 effectively made this essential environment an impossibility.

"I remember I was hosting a 1,700-seat event at the ARTSCAPE Theatre in Cape Town, South Africa. I jumped on one of the last flights out of Cape Town before the pandemic started shutting down borders and international flights. By the time I landed, the news was pretty certain: in-person events weren't happening for a while.

"Initially, I was thrilled. I had this poorly-paying gig in Colchester that upcoming Monday that I wasn't looking forward to. Now I didn't have to go; I got my Monday night back!" Stu's delight at not having to reckon with the relentless demands of a life on the road was short-lived once the gravity of the pandemic was apparent.

"Many comics have income that isn't so reliant on live shows. Some write for TV shows or have plans to write a book. Among my fellow stand-ups, I am very oriented on the live show. Frankly, I was lucky to have the podcast for as long as I did at that point."

To go from hosting events at a 1,700-seat theatre to staring at his bedroom walls, Stu knew he had to figure a way to maintain his income while still appealing to the audiences who loved his live shows. This situation might have crushed other performers who made their livings by booking rooms and mic nights, but Stu knew he could rely on the resilience he developed through the years.

"I knew I could exploit my network. The 'insiders' who subscribed to my podcast were very "sticky" listeners and enjoyed the way my mind works as much as they enjoyed my comedy output. They were a small-ish group compared to some comics' vast followings, but I knew I could count on them as I started to test out new things."

Other comedians were similarly vexed. "There were a couple of wars on different fronts," according to Bob DiBuono, a headlining comedian who had been doing stand-up for more than 20 years. "No. 1 is comedians are independent contractors. We make a living with each show that we do. It's a huge financial blow for comics because there's nowhere for a long time to perform. And then secondly, artistically and creatively, just like an athlete who has to go out every day and practice a jump shot or get in the batting cage, an artist, especially a comedian, you have to be out there all the time, constantly working out the material." It was an extremely challenging time for anyone reliant on comedy for a living.

Stu's forays into the business world had introduced him to the use of agile thinking and planning to put new ideas into practice. After some creative thinking, he realised he could replicate a live stand-up show's "audience feel" if the audience could still see one another. If there is one thing that we all discovered throughout the lockdowns, it is that we got to know each other rather well through Zoom. Using the platform, Stu first trialled a game show where contestants had to complete a certain task for time or else they would get kicked out of the coveted Zoom call. Stu then experimented with a live chat show called *The Infinite Sofa*. He gathered 12 punters in a Zoom room and let them join in interviewing three comics over 90 minutes. Stu hosted *The Infinite Sofa* every Monday and Wednesday during the lockdowns, and it was watched on Twitch by hundreds of thousands of viewers.

"I eventually got the feel that all the stuff we were doing online was like the Edinburgh Fringe that went on 24/7. Performers showed up and were game to do things if they had something to promote," Stu said.

During the pandemic, Stu still managed to do 30 shows, including a Glastonbury special and a Machynlleth comedy special. "It was all exhausting. Fun, but exhausting. Sometimes we'd get a pretty decent pay-out, and I was grateful for some regular micro-donations, but it couldn't sustain me financially."

Then Stu shifted into corporate shows - something that turned out to be very lucrative. Reaching out to the network he had developed in his public speaking career, he started booking *The Infinite Sofa* as a holiday special for corporate clients. They had the revenue; he had the model, so why not? "It was such new and unknown territory. I didn't have a roadmap or a producer; there was no boss or agent to be responsible to. I had to learn to shrug off my doubts. Was a set too in-jokey, or not in-jokey enough? Am I swearing too much for this particular client? Or is the anarchic nature of comedy the thing they wanted the most?"

While the corporate gigs and online shows paid the bills, they didn't scratch the itch. "At the time, I didn't realise that I was motivated by my desperation. I always felt like I HAD to do these shows to maintain the momentum of my career. I started realising that the work that was available wasn't necessarily the work I wanted to be doing." It was extremely difficult work having to book, script, and produce two chat shows every week in addition to outside gigs and mentoring. Also: parenting. Stu's family needed his attention and support during the entire ordeal. "How do you give yourself a chance to rest and remember what is important when you've cultivated this mode of instantly saying 'yes' to everything?"

In the act of self-preservation, Stu cut the public chat shows and focused entirely on the corporate shows. "It was kind of scary, I felt this enormous guilt that I was somehow letting down the core audience that had shown up and supported the online shows over all these months." But this was the essence of resilience that comics were known for. It's not about being able to do absolutely everything but knowing how to make the most of certain opportunities so you can keep showing up for what matters day after day. Stu got better at delegating tasks that he wasn't so great at so he could better deliver on what he was good for.

"Looking back, I know I was incredibly lucky. The career I had built before the pandemic allowed me to take risks. I had some income that allowed me to pivot and deliberately diversify what I was doing," says Stu. The resilience combined with the improvisational nature of comedy meant he could experiment with all kinds of things. Ask any stand-up, and they'll tell you your entire job is learning to try again, fail again, and go with what works. Embrace the failure, and then move forward. "You soon learn that your family and fans are a rock-solid foundation of support." This positive attitude and being agile and innovative enabled Stu to survive and thrive during the pandemic. His business improved and is now healthier and more robust than ever, and he was more resilient and confident about what came next.

The live shows are back, and Stu is back doing them. He still regularly updates his podcast, has retained some components of his online show, and has learnt a lot about social media and video content. His resilience through the pandemic has made him busier than ever in the post-pandemic world, as his keynotes have gone from strength to strength. Recently, he developed a new keynote on coping with eco-anxiety; he too has seen the link between lessons from the pandemic and the climate crisis. Following the pandemic, he feels ready for whatever the world might throw at him next. Stu has retained the online performance element and can now perform gigs live and online, enabling him to maintain a bigger programme of shows and perform for people worldwide without travelling. He has the tools now to reach a global population and to change the world.

And he's also writing a book. I'd like to think he's inspired by this one. (hah!) :D

"Darkness cannot drive out darkness: only light can do that. Hate cannot drive out hate: only love can do that."
— Martin Luther King Jr.

Chapter Three

Rowing The Void

The elite rowing squad, forced to train out of the boat and in isolation for a race that might not take place, building a team culture and ultimately winning the race while also studying at a prestigious university.

T HROUGH THE YEARS, THE results have been relatively neck and neck - 85 Cambridge wins to Oxford's 81 with only one draw in 1877. Those taking part compete to win and to be a part of something bigger than themselves. The Boat Race has occurred annually since 1829 and pits the Cambridge University rowing crew against the Oxford University crew. Fans from all over the world attend and watch live or from their televisions, but The Boat Race is still an amateur event organised and run by volunteers with limited budgets. Of course, a win boosts the team's morale. However, crews must find a way to get to the start line with a winning mindset to stand a chance of winning. And that's exactly what the Cambridge University Boat Club (CUBC) discovered during the pandemic. They were considered underdogs compared to a strong Oxford crew and had to overcome the added challenges of enduring intense training through the lockdowns of 2020 and 2021.

The rowing culture around Cambridge and Oxford is immense. The Boat Race is the hallmark event for the UK, pitting two rival teams against one another across a 6.8km stretch of water - significantly more than any Olympic or World Championship course. But beyond The Boat Race, it is estimated that nearly 400,000 people across the UK row for sport or leisure. This population supports a larger ecosystem of boat builders, manufacturers, equipment retailers, rowing courses, river stewardship, volunteers, umpires, and coaches.

Rob Baker has been rowing for as long as he can remember. Through the years, he has been a sculler, rower, and elite coach for international teams - the sport runs in his blood. He married a rower. His father was a rower. At this point, he has likely spent most of his life on rivers rowing and coaching. Today he is the head coach of CUBC and coaches athletes for the Great Britain rowing team. I know Rob from when I rowed as a Cambridge junior and a University rower. We've kept in touch ever since, and I've watched his successful coaching career and shared his passion for elite sport, particularly rowing. Quinten Richardson started rowing at Shawnigan Lake School on Vancouver Island, where he eventually would compete at an international level. He would be one of the strongest additions to the Brown University rowing crew. After graduating with an undergrad degree, Quinten took a break from studies and started his career. After several years, Quinten would continue his rowing career while working on his master's degree in urban planning at Cambridge. Joining the CUBC meant Quinten would be one of the older rowers on the team, but this meant he would connect well with Rob and serve as a natural leader for the team.

The rowing culture at Cambridge was starting to make some changes at the end of 2019; the club was looking to enhance its approach to funding and training the rowing teams. They had consolidated the university's three rowing clubs (CUBC, Cambridge University's Women's Boat Club, and the Lightweight rowing club) into one co-ed, all-weight club that would represent Cambridge against Oxford. All of these efforts focused on beating Oxford, including increasing the recruiting efforts to bring the best rowers in the world to Cambridge. The 2020/ 2021 year was no exception. To focus on their efforts and build team camaraderie, six members of the men's team with international pedigree – including Quinten – rented a house on Abbey Road in Cambridge during the summer of 2020, ultimately christening it "The Abbey." This is the moment the teams started trialling and testing for the 2021 race.

All around the world, Elite sporting events were cancelled or postponed indefinitely. Social distancing protocols not only put a hold on spectator events, but practice matches and training sessions were also tricky to navigate. Unfortunately, the 2020 Boat Race was cancelled two weeks before the start of the event. When Rob started to prepare for the 2021 race, it was thought that the pandemic was behind us. But as of August 2020, the coronavirus flared up again. Along with the rest of the UK, The Abbey went into lockdown in November 2020, effectively shutting down everything important to the team. Not only the races but also the time spent in the training facilities and the opportunities to row together. They were in and out of lockdown for the remainder of the run up to the race, all the while having to continually update and adapt their training regiments.

And now six very large, very active, elite student-athletes were enclosed in a small house with no idea how long the quarantine would last. They couldn't get on the water with teammates locked down elsewhere. Since they couldn't train together in the gym, they brought the gym to The Abbey and started their winter-style training early. The entire team, including those not housed at The Abbey, had rowing machines delivered to their houses and weights to build their own training centre. Just like every other organisation at the time, team meetings were held over Zoom. And while Zoom meetings could never replace in-person training, the connections allowed the team to continue to bond and make decisions together. Studies were starting to emerge on the impact of COVID-19 infection among elite athletes. Doctors observed that most elite athletes only experienced mild symptoms and were usually back to sport in about two weeks, possibly due to their athleticism. But in some cases, it could take several months to come back due to the lingering effects, so the team didn't take any chances. They kept their distance, held each other accountable, and created a positive energy from which the rest of the crew fed.

All the while, they were still studying for their classes, cooking, eating, and maintaining The Abbey. They trained in the garden, they ate, and they studied. Before long, the Groundhog Day effect set in. Combined with the dreary winter of January 2021, depression started to set in with some of the teammates.

"We kept up a shared spreadsheet for each squad member to put in their rowing times and what they did for weight-training sessions. If someone didn't fill in for a few days, we checked in on them to ensure they were alright. Depression can really drain you," Quinten says. "And Rob was a huge influence in how we responded to the pandemic." These inter-team communications were key to ensuring everyone on the team could see the light through the darkness - sometimes, that meant having to be the light for one another.

Cambridge would need to row at their absolute best to stand a chance against a much stronger Oxford crew on paper and have to perform exceptionally to beat them. Over the Zoom calls, Rob would remind the team, "I can't row the race for you, but if you row as you only know how, we're sure to win this." The training continued. At The Abbey, the team maintained its morale by bringing out musical instruments and jamming. They spent time cooking for each other and bonding around mealtimes at the kitchen table. The neighbours soon learned there was a house full of elite athletes living and training just steps from their doorway. All the while, no one was certain if there was even a race to compete in. It takes a certain kind of athlete to train even when there is potentially nothing to train for, and the CUBC crew had exactly this mindset.

They would watch movies at The Abbey on their rest days. The wider team were doing the same. One movie in particular that Rob watched - *Touching The Void* - inspired the team. The movie was an account of two climbers enduring a challenging expedition in Patagonia. In the film, one of the climbers recounts how he made the journey by reducing his efforts to focusing on getting to the next rock, and then the rock after that, and so on. The climber moved a few meters at a time until he reached the journey's end. This idea became something of a mantra for the team. Crucial parts of the race plan were "the next rock".

The uncertainty as to whether the race would take place continued. Not knowing whether their main event of the season would be on or when it would take place made training programmes almost impossible to plan. Every sport faced this challenge. The European Championships Football tournament was delayed by an entire year.

The 2020 summer tournament didn't happen until the summer of 2021. This threw training protocols into chaos, and coping with the uncertainty was mentally draining.

Then the announcement came: the race was on. It was happening not on The Thames in London, but in Ely on a stretch of the River Ouse near Cambridge. The event would be limited to athletes - no spectators. The team used the time to make final preparations. 10 days before the race, the entire crew moved into separate cottages for COVID-19 quarantine protocols. Rob says: "My vision was to ensure the crew had time to bond as a cohesive team as we approached race day. This meant I had to get out of the way. I told them they were responsible for how they were going to run the race."

The crew unrolled a meters-long piece of paper across the table where they planned out every single stroke of the race. From the starting push to where they would go for an all-out sprint. They broke down the entire course into 150-meter sections they called "rocks." All they had to do was get to the next rock. Rob reviewed the paper roll, made a few suggestions, and was ultimately satisfied with the plan.

"That plan was a key element of the race," Rob said. "Or, rather, the act of planning it out was. They were thinking about all the different ways the race could play out. What would they do if they were ahead? Or if Oxford pulled ahead?" Looking at the stats, Oxford proved to be a superior crew that year and was favoured to win. The plan on the roll of paper levelled the playing field.

The CUBC crew gathered for a pre-race warm-up on the day of the race. Here, Rob addressed the team. He opened up about his trials during the pandemic and the previous year's challenges and that his father was diagnosed with terminal cancer. This was the first time the rest of the crew was aware of this. Rob shared how he had coped with all of this while also coaching the team and ensuring they were prepared for the race. "But that's all this is, just a race," Rob said to put everything in perspective. It had been a long year, a long road, and the journey itself had benefited everyone no matter how the race turned out.

The carefully constructed plan - The Rocks - didn't survive the first 100 meters. The energy and enthusiasm of being back in the boat with the team took over. The plan was to row hard, settle into a cadence, and then push again. But the crew had gone off from the start way harder than planned. By 500m, Cambridge was ahead of Oxford by a full boat length. Then they were clear of them by the 1KM mark, but the team was burning too much energy. Quinten remembers: "Once we passed the 3km mark, I could feel like I was in the red zone. I wasn't sure I could maintain the cadence." His arms burned, his breath was heavy, and Oxford was starting to gain on their boat.

"I remember the cox telling the crew to think of the rocks. Get to the next rock. Then the next one," Quinten recounted. More than this, this is where the team culture made all the difference. No one wanted to let their teammates down. Having got to this point, having worked for years getting here, overcoming the challenges of the pandemic, they were not going to let the dream go now. Lives flashed before the Cambridge crew as they looked back at Oxford. Cambridge were straining every sinew to maintain the lead. Years of work had gone into this moment. In just a few months, they had come such a huge way in bonding and building as a team. The pandemic had brought even more intensity to this, acting as a pressure cooker. Memories of training together. Of being outside in the backyard in the snow and the rain. The shared experience had become hugely powerful to draw from in the race. Against all the odds, Cambridge maintained their lead over Oxford and finished the race just 2 seconds ahead.

Cambridge had won. Over the broadcast, announcers were astonished by what they had seen.

"That was one of the most extraordinary performances I've ever seen on that stretch of water. There is just something special about this crew; they really gelled together."

There were several ingredients to the victory. Through high levels of uncertainty, the crew's positive, purpose-led attitude enabled them to maintain focus and intensity in training and arrive at the start line in the right shape and with the right mentality. "Leadership made this all happen," Quinten recalls. Rob says: "It's not my style to micromanage. I'm just here to empower the crew and create an environment of trust." Rob sometimes wondered if being physically separate from the team while most of the crew lived in The Abbey gave them a sense of self-reliance. "Whatever it was, I'm not sure I would have done anything different." They both agree that the pandemic brought out the best in the Cambridge crew. The crew might not have won if it hadn't been for the pandemic. The core of the crew wouldn't have been in the same house. They wouldn't have met each other or bonded as they did. They wouldn't have built the culture. It was all a part of the virtuous cycle of training, improving, bonding and, through it all, even managing to have fun with it.

As lockdown measures have decreased, the club has largely returned to their pre-pandemic approach to training. When rowing with a crew, nothing can substitute being with your mates out on the water. But a huge amount was learnt from the pandemic race on the Ouse at Ely. For many of our clients, COVID-19 pushed leaders and their teams to innovate. This was borne out of necessity, but often the ideas were things that they had been thinking about trying before but not had the courage to try. The pandemic forced the ideas into practice. CUBC hasn't abandoned all of the pandemic adjustments. They still use video conferencing to keep in touch with the team, and a teammate's overall wellness is now more of a focus. And more than ever, they recognise the importance of building a winning team with a purpose and attitude to maximise their chances of beating their age-old rivals.

"We can easily forgive a child who is afraid of the dark; the real tragedy of life is when men are afraid of the light."
— Plato

Chapter Four

Banking On The Team

How a European digital bank survived the shock of the pandemic and thrived by fostering a culture of collaboration to establish a new platform for growth.

I F YOUR BUSINESS HAD a consumer-facing retail front, it likely faced an exceptional challenge during the peak days of COVID-19. If you weren't an international eCommerce giant that has grown its dominance over the past twenty years, you likely had to jump a few new hurdles as governments and unions determined how businesses could safely run during a global pandemic. This is the challenge Arnaud Denis faced as the CEO of MeDirect - a pan-European challenger bank headquartered in Malta.

While Arnaud's background is primarily in financial and banking services, he had initial experience in the French Military. His time in national service included an education at the Special Military School of Saint-Cyr, an academy created by Napoleon Bonaparte in 1800. Since its inception, over 65,000 cadets have been trained under the motto: *Ils s'instruisent pour vaincre* - They Study to Overcome (or, depending on the translator, conquer or win. They are, after all, a military academy). Since graduating from Saint-Cyr, Arnaud has worked for over 25 years in the financial service industry for institutions across Europe. He spent the majority of his time working internationally, becoming comfortable working across the world, in US, Asia and Eastern Europe. Since 2013, Arnaud has led companies from the C-suite, acquiring experience in driving change and turnarounds at an international scale. These skills were a perfect match for when he stepped in as CEO at MeDirect in 2019.

Arnaud and the MeDirect team are close connections and clients of Key & Co. The bank is a longstanding client and we know the business well through our involvement in the strategy and transformation of their business for a few years. Previously, MeDirect was known as Mediterranean Bank, which was acquired by AnaCap Financial Partners LLP (a private equity fund based out of the UK) in 2009. In the years since the acquisition, the bank saw significant growth in its home country of Malta where the staff of 330 uses cutting edge technology to serve many clients.

One of the notable expansions of the business was moving into the Belgium market as an online bank that offered significant consumer savings, investments, and wealth management services. MeDirect became a fully licensed Belgian bank in 2015. By 2019 they had also moved into the Dutch and Malta mortgage markets. While this seems like an incredible growth and reach, the company has managed to stay agile with its eye on a high-growth trajectory to disrupt the banking industry. As of July 2022, MeDirect served over 100,000 customers and had a book of over 4.5 billion euros in assets, including a 1.7 billion euro mortgage book. They built this through their accessible WealthTech platform, allowing customers with typically €30-100k in financial assets to manage their wealth and investments without relying on a financial manager. Arnaud saw this as a vast yet underserved market, the long tail of the wealth management opportunity.

"MeDirect's goal as a Wealth Tech is to democratise investing by creating a unique Wealth Super App that offers a broad range of online investment solutions to retail clients who are looking for simplicity, transparency, and personalisation. A Wealth SuperApp that can also be used to serve everyday banking needs."

Going into 2020, MeDirect had a clear growth strategy for the year ahead. While many companies were left scrambling to adjust in the mire of the pandemic, MeDirect already had a plan in place that was further validated by the onset of the crisis. In fact, the actions around their vision and purpose are what helped them accelerate through the pandemic.

While many businesses had a "global pandemic" on their risk register, very few thought it would happen, including MeDirect. In the year leading up to the COVID-19 pandemic, MeDirect experienced radical changes and growth, all due to the ongoing development of its core digital proposition for underserved customers. The goal was to increase their reach to retail customers in European countries beyond Belgium and Malta. Arnaud knew the economic implications of the pandemic would show up in the customer's finances. A lot of people have personal challenges with money and their future financial security. Plus, with every other headline being a reminder of the grim reality we were all facing, MeDirect employees had to keep their banks running. Fortunately, by this point, the bank already knew the strength of their agility and they were led by someone who had *studied to overcome*.

In early July 2020, Malta could boast of being the country with the fewest number of active cases of coronavirus in the whole of the EU. Throughout the early part of the pandemic, the island was the darling of the World Health Organisation, which had praised the health authority's COVID-19 containment strategy. But within weeks, Malta has seen such a dramatic increase in coronavirus patients that it entered the top ten European countries for the number of new COVID-19 cases for every 100,000 people.

Of course, MeDirect had to make changes when the pandemic struck. Within a week of the shutdown, every employee had the equipment necessary to work remotely. In fact, a Key & Co. team was working with them when the lockdown struck and had to race back from Belgium on the last train back to the UK before lockdown. The safety and welfare of MeDirect employees were paramount to everything. New hires were onboarded virtually with daily training and education in conflict resolution and mental resilience. The technology team was very busy, averaging eight releases a day between January 2021 and May 2022. With such a quick shift, MeDirect was in a great position to keep transforming the landscape of banking and wealth management. In 2020, they launched a new mobile app, revamped their eBanking platform, and rolled out customer onboarding for new customers. Between their clear plan and agile team, MeDirect went from a £65M loss in 2020 to a substantial profit in 2022 – an incredible achievement.

"We had to maintain a strong momentum on our priorities, even accelerating a number of strategic initiatives. As a result, we continued to grow in our key areas - like Dutch residential mortgages and digital wealth services. At the same time, the bank had to manage its financial performance and balance sheet ruthlessly. As a result, in 2020, we reported a total capital ratio of 17.3%, well beyond what was required by regulators."

Despite the intense pressures, MeDirect weathered the pandemic. Arnaud had the combined challenges of keeping a business on track and leading the team. His employees faced increased stress and were exhausted by working through difficult circumstances that were relentless, initially thinking they would be doing so for a few weeks but ultimately continuing for more than two years. They had to school their children remotely or look after family with health conditions while having a universal concern for their job. On top of it all: the isolation of working remotely. Staying positive throughout was immensely challenging but critical to maintaining a motivated team and overcoming fatigue.

By doubling down the online business and equipping the workforce to work remotely, MeDirect kept its customers finances secure. Still, it was the further investment in the workforce that was critical to keeping them motivated and engaged. All managers and business owners learned during the pandemic that there is no simple solution to resolving employee stress amid a pandemic. It's not the sort of thing they teach you in business school.

Other businesses also discovered how the pandemic accelerated their transformation around technology. According to a recent survey of IT decision-makers by eFax, 60% of businesses are accelerating the speed of their transformation projects as a direct result of the disruption the pandemic wrought on their workforces, and it's no different for banks. An EY study found that 43% of consumers say the way they bank has changed due to COVID-19 – with a particular emphasis on moving from physical contact (including limiting trips to branches and shifting away from using cash) to more digital channels.

One thing Arnaud focused on was the team-mentality. An ethos of teamwork meant that everyone worked together to navigate the crisis - both on a business and personal front. When the team stays together, they keep each other motivated and are each other's light in the darkness. They can also be the light for their customers. The personal situation of MeDirect's customers may have been in flux, but MeDirect could give them control over their finances and the confidence to manage their wealth through the crisis.

Despite a global pandemic, the company provided exceptional support to its clients and communities. Agility was central to this. While bigger banks were having issues pivoting, laying off staff, and even going under, MeDirect saw progress toward all their strategic goals - like a 165% increase in the WealthTech business and a 50% growth in the mortgage business in 2021. Now on the other side of the pandemic, the company can only grow from there.

With a renewed sense of confidence and strength in the business, MeDirect revamped its brand in 2022 to focus on a better customer experience and to bridge the gaps between old and new models of the banking sector. The crisis meant that MeDirect had no time to rest on its laurels. When you get comfortable in your everyday job, a crisis is the exact thing you may need to shake up your business and show where the imbalances are hiding. MeDirect also benefited from its size. When crises happen, bigger is not always better. Global banks like Citibank - with 200,000 employees and numerous retail branches – had significant challenges adapting to the challenges of the pandemic. No matter how large your organisation is, when the variables change, you must change with them. Being positive, agile, and working effectively as a team sets up MeDirect to stand strong for future challenges.

"It is often in the darkest skies that we see the brightest stars."
— Richard Evans

Chapter Five

The Beacon Of Hope

In a time when one's faith was tested, churches worldwide had to close their doors as communities went into lockdown. One church leader used technology to amplify the message to the world and remind his congregation that the church is more than just a building, and that one's faith can grow wherever one happens to be.

THROUGH THE GOOD TIMES and the bad, the church has always served as a bastion of faith for people all over the world. St. James' Church in London has been a beacon of hope for the community since the original building was constructed in 1829. The community, like the building, always finds its way through the darkness, even when it is shaken from its very foundation.

Today, St. James' is led by their Vicar, Reverend Kit Gunasekera. As the fifteenth vicar over the history of the church, and now in his fourteenth year, Kit knows the church's role in the surrounding community. Born in London and of Sri Lankan descent, Kit spent his early childhood in his family's culture in the capital city of Colombo. It wasn't until he turned 17 that Kit discovered his faith and pursued a study of theology at Cambridge University. In 2006 he was ordained.

Kit's mission through St. James' Church is simple: "know Christ and make Him known." His days are spent helping and enabling this mission to happen in the communities with which he and the church are linked. Kit's vision for the church is ambitious; he wants it to be an ever-growing community of prayerful people of all ages and backgrounds who love God and their neighbours. The church, with its history and splendour, is the building enabling his vision. These ambitions led the church to support the Clapham Park Foodbank in its effort to provide food relief for those in crisis. St. James' has worked with The Robes Project to provide meals and a warm place to sleep during the winter for those who find themselves unhoused. At Harvest, they also support the Ace of Clubs, which ensures those who live on the forgotten margins of society have food, care, and the support they need.

Overall, the parish of St. James' works to be a good neighbour in the community. Kit, ably supported by fellow clergy Revd John Marshall, Revd John Ohen, and a team of willing and hard-working lay volunteers, make these efforts possible even as the number of self-reporting Christians is in decline. While over half the population of the UK has a relationship with their local church (upwards of 30 million people), church patronage has been in steady decline in the UK. Since

2011, the number of identifying Christians in the UK has declined by approximately 13% - from 33.3 million to 27.5 million. Churches still have a strong presence in communities, but they struggle with engaging their parishioners in an age that feels like everything is getting faster and busier by the day.

A church is built on community and connection, on loving your neighbour by knowing all that makes them unique - something that happens naturally with regular gatherings. In 2019, St. James' welcomed about 50 people to its pews each Sunday. This group was ethnically diverse and spoke to the transient nature of the congregation. Kit and his team would preach from under the gorgeously vibrant stained glass window that faces east and filters the sunrise each morning. Between their insightful words of wisdom, the prayer, and the colours of the glass, the congregation always has something to look forward to every week.

But with social gatherings becoming a high-transmission risk, churches worldwide had to close their doors to their congregations - something no pastor, priest, or vicar could ever imagine doing. Yet, the unimaginable happened as the pandemic quickly extended its global reach. Kit had to close the doors of St. James', and his congregation was left without a place to gather. While the pandemic was unprecedented, St. James' had faced adversity before. At 2:15 AM on September 6th, 1940, the entire church was reduced to rubble during the Battle of Britain. During the Second World War, German forces attempted to force the United Kingdom into surrender through a drawn-out campaign of air raids and bombings. While the campaign initially focused on military targets, it wasn't long before the attackers started laying indiscriminate siege to political and civilian targets.

St. James' was a victim of one of those indiscriminate attacks. While the church and the surrounding city blocks were decimated, the community kept calm and carried on as the bombings continued for another two months. As the war ended and the dust settled, the congregation set to rebuilding the church and the community. The congregation met in other spaces to restore their faith and support one another while they rebuilt their formal church. Over a century later, in 1958, the most recent construction of the St. James' Church - with its brilliant stained glass window - was completed.

If the congregation could survive wartime attacks, it could certainly find a way to support one another during a time of pandemic.

"Zoom was a saviour," Kit says with little irony. For it was his wife, Jill, who introduced Kit and the church to Zoom. Like millions of communities worldwide, video conferencing technology was essential to maintaining a sense of normalcy during the pandemic. It started as weekly services delivered over Zoom into the living rooms of the congregation. The digital communication extended to ensuring the church could still support the Ace of Clubs and the Clapham Park Food Bank - all of whom saw a drastically increased demand as the pandemic rocked the economy and threatened individuals' food and income security.

Kit still took funerals and weddings where he could. However, new opportunities to meet online were made evident as the pandemic lockdown dragged on. A Wednesday morning coffee and chat, Morning and Night Prayers, a quiz sent via email, children and youth group meetings, and bible studies all moved online. While nothing could replace in-person meetings, each digital connection with a member of his church was a reminder that physical humanness still existed on the other side of the screen. Although Kit found the experience personally challenging as he couldn't be there to celebrate the highs or mourn the lows of his flock, he could still create new ways for the congregation to connect and worship. St. James is on my street; I can see it from my house. I am not a regular churchgoer, but I did become one during the pandemic. I joined the Zoom church services and got to know Kit and his congregation well. It was fascinating to observe how Kit led a community of people through this period.

Eventually, the restrictions loosened, and the congregation felt it safe to return to the church. Through it all, Kit knows his faith, and the faith of his followers, has only strengthened. The pandemic highlighted the cracks in the surrounding community and revealed ways the congregation could provide further support. And while people have now returned to the building for services - and to admire the stained glass window – Kit still broadcasts over Zoom to reach worshipers who are housebound or ill, or even if they are tuning in from the other side of the world. A technological solution came from the pandemic that was needed all along – a way to bring people together who want to participate, even if they cannot leave their homes.

Before the pandemic, several studies in the UK had highlighted the impact of loneliness, which may have a similar impact on mortality as smoking, drinking, or obesity. During the lockdowns, we had to find ways to maintain social connections and communities like St. James all over the world looked for innovative ways to achieve this.

According to Stephen Reicher, a member of the Sage subcommittee advising on behavioural science in the UK, writing in the Guardian, there has been a remarkable growth of social solidarity during the pandemic, with well over 4,000 mutual aid groups forming up and down the country and over 12 million people engaged in volunteering (of whom some 5 million were first-time volunteers). Such groups have provided critical services that the state could never duplicate: checking to see if people are OK, delivering food, and even walking the dog.

Even as it has distanced us from loved ones, the pandemic has also brought us closer together in other ways. The shared crisis experience has forged a greater sense of unity at the street, neighbourhood and even national level. It has backed up the research that suggests that a sense of belonging to communities can protect people against depression, improve cognition in older people, dramatically improve people's health prospects on retirement and greatly improve recovery from heart attacks. Our membership in groups and communities is its own type of "social cure".

This isn't just a story about how Zoom kept people connected, but a reminder that the connection is a far second compared to the importance of *purpose*. Broadcasting services are the most visible output, but maintaining a connection to your community and ensuring those within are safe and cared for is where the real work happens. However, while technology may show the world your altar, but having a positive approach to the situation puts the power behind the broadcast. Like the businesses we worked with during the pandemic, remaining positive, even through the most challenging times, was essential for St. James to navigate the crisis. Kit reflects on the pandemic: "out of an unprecedented time of restrictions, fear, and loss, new ways of being church and community emerged, and I think as a church, we are closer to each other and to our local community than before." Even in the hardest times, you must stick to your purpose and vision to see the light that will guide you through the darkness.

"It's so much darker when a light goes out than it would have been if it had never shone."

— John Steinbeck

Chapter Six

Always A Reason To Celebrate

Unable to imagine a world without cake, a local baker finds inspiration and changes her business recipe to bring her kitchen bakery to a global audience.

At her wedding to the Prince Albert of Saxe-Coburg, Queen Victoria had her celebratory cake frosted with white icing – she was one of the first to do it, and the resulting confection is known today as "Royal Icing." I know this because Holly Barea knows this, and her cakes have graced the tables of royalty and celebrities all across London. Holly takes about 350 cake orders through her company – Etoile Bakery – every year for everything from edible centrepieces at stylish weddings to special birthdays celebrated with loved ones. "One of my clients is a Saudi oil baron, and his orders are always huge! Always well into the thousands." And Holly runs Etoile Bakery from her home kitchen, where she bakes the week's cakes in batches, allowing days for proper cooling and elaborate decorating before they are delivered to neighbourhoods all around London. She tells me that the "secret" to a great cake is to use soft butter and bake it at lower temperatures.

And to think, Holly and her cakes almost vanished in an instant. As with so many businesses, the early days of the COVID-19 lockdown had Holly wondering how she would manage to keep baking. You might not have realised it then, but Etoile Bakery is one of those businesses we didn't first think of as essential. But given its creative foundations and Holly's backstory, it is almost impossible to imagine a world without cake.

In a previous life, Holly worked for Industrial Credit and Investment Corporation of India (ICICI), a private bank headquartered in Mumbai with branches worldwide. She quickly realised she was not suited for a typical office job, especially with the travel demands and wanting to spend time with her two children. Thinking back to her childhood and the cakes her mother made, Holly was inspired to create unique and spectacular works of art with sugar, butter, and flour. Heeding the call of her creative nature and entrepreneurial desires, Holly enrolled in the Cordon Bleu School in London. By 2012 she was running Etoile Bakery out of her home kitchen and baking cakes for customers throughout South London. In 2013 she was awarded the "Best Party Supplier" in London and received noted customer service awards in 2016.

Holly's and my children went to school together, and my wife and I are friends with Holly and her husband. I have followed Holly's successes as Etoile Bakery grew steadily over the years. During this time, we often connected to share our experiences with starting and growing our respective businesses. Before long, she had to hire an assistant to handle some of the baking duties in her out kitchen and a support staffer to handle everything from administration to deliveries. As 2019 ended and they looked ahead to 2020, Holly focused on expanding the business, hiring more staff, working more parties and weddings – the very lifeblood of her business – and leaning in on the face-to-face element of her business. 2020 would be a year for growth!

But you can already guess where this story goes.

Holly always made time to meet with friends and family, and they even joked that the looming pandemic shutdown might mean they wouldn't see each other for a year. Little did they know that it would be at least that long before she was in the same room as some of her favourite people again.

The virus spread, the lockdowns began, and Holly's business vanished overnight. Or so it seemed. Why bother with an elaborate cake if you can't have a party? Like so many other business owners, Holly watched as her business practically fell off a cliff as customers called in to cancel their orders. The isolation protocols meant her assistant couldn't work out of her kitchen – even if there was work to do in the first place.

These circumstances left Holly with two weeks of thinking: "OK, now what?" She had kids to put through school, a mortgage to pay, bills that needed paying, and zero business revenue coming in. With nothing but time on her hands; Holly toyed with business ideas she had had on the back burner over the years. Would one of them result in the income her family needed?

Holly's business was in a particularly challenging situation, as both a small business and operating within the hospitality sector, which lost £200M per day in the UK in 2020 due to COVID-19 restrictions. And running a small business through the pandemic was extremely stressful, particularly for women. A May 2020 poll by Gallup compared small business owners' stress and worry levels before COVID-19 and during it. Both male and female participants reported rises in those things during the pandemic, but the effects were especially severe for women. 38% of females experienced daily stress in pre-COVID times, but 62% did at the time of the study.

As the shock of the shutdown faded into the "new normal," Holly set to work on the things she should have done over the years, even if it was only a matter of having something to do. Like many of us during the pandemic, she turned her attention to social media. On Instagram, she started sharing cookbooks she loved and recipes she was working on, all the while slowly building an audience. Still, the monotony set in as it did with many entrepreneurs. She missed the challenge of being busy and delivering fantastic client results. Most of all, she missed having something to look forward to – a holiday, a party, a special event, or a vacation. All of this, combined with managing the remote learning of her two teenage children, Holly was dealt quite a hand.

Then, out of nowhere, the orders started coming back in. As a food producer, Etoile Bakery was allowed to reopen and operate during the pandemic. Even in lockdown, people still needed cake. Although it could be argued that everyone could use a cake at just about any time, the isolationist feeling of a quarantine made every anniversary and celebration memorable. The market for smaller, individual cakes and cupcakes replaced her usual orders for a single large cake that might have been ordered for a birthday party. Each guest received their own mini-cake to enjoy as they celebrated through Zoom. Employers sent cakes as appreciation gifts to their employees enduring the pandemic in their homes. Where Etoile Bakery had primarily oriented itself to events typically held on the weekend, Holly noticed an increased demand in the "mid-week" orders. There is always a reason for a good bit of cake, especially on a Wednesday!

As with anything for a business owner, especially during the age of the pandemic, getting back on track wasn't so easy. Cake orders were coming in, but acquiring the ingredients to fulfil them proved challenging with the ongoing supply chain issues. Butter and eggs were hard to come by, and the food-safe cardboard she used to package the cakes was in short supply. Since the grocery stores and food markets were rationing ingredients like eggs and butter, Holly would send in her teenage children separately to purchase additional quantities of what they needed.

Holly's supply chain challenges were like many other small businesses. A survey of more than 100,000 small business owners in the United States examined COVID-19's impact on supply chains, among other things. The results indicated that 45% of overall businesses reported supply chain disruptions. However, the total climbed to 66% in retail, 61% in health care and social assistance and 50% in manufacturing

Delivering numerous individual-sized cakes meant more time in the car. While London may be world-renown for its traffic, the shutdown meant far fewer people were out and about on those days. The delivery process first gave Holly an eerie feeling – the empty roads, the closed shops, the lack of people – but seeing her customers only solidified the critical nature of Etoile Bakery's role in the community. Not only were the deliveries essential to the business's survival, but the presence of a beautiful cake reminded everyone that there was always a reason to celebrate, even in the dark times.

Then came the biggest shift in the business: the launch of Etoile Bakery's online cooking course.

With her husband Lawrence behind the camera (and in the editing suite), Holly walked her patrons through how to bake and ice their own cakes. This turned Etoile Bakery from a local business into a global one. Local customers got an inside look at how Holly made her magic, while international students gained access to expertise that wasn't previously available in their area. It was an entirely new way for Etoile Bakery to connect with its customers that was both engaging and lucrative.

The lockdowns eventually ended. Places reopened, and people ventured out into the world they had been deprived of for months on end. The UK returned to "normal" fairly quickly, and the core of Etoile Bakery's regular business returned with it. Post-pandemic, Holly is running an expanded business compared to before. The market for online learning courses has since saturated, meaning the online baking school levelled off, but the in-person events have taken right off again. The face-to-face festivities postponed during the lockdown have come back in full force and with it, all the reasons to have a stunning cake at the centre of everything. The lockdown-driven shift to improving her online presence, a seemingly arbitrary task at the time, has delivered an increased customer base and a reason to develop new parts of her business, which likely left her better prepared to jump back into the action once things opened up.

Returning to "normal" doesn't mean the business is without challenges. The compounded issues of the pandemic years – supply chain issues, global inflation, and shifts in the economy – have driven up the cost of living and the price of goods in the UK. Some of Holly's customers have taken a second look as to where their discretionary spending goes. However, Etoile Bakery maintains its focus on the higher-end luxury market, and Holly always keeps future ventures in her sights. Including, potentially, a brick-and-mortar store or baking school.

The ability to innovate and the agility to pivot to reinvent the business were critical in the survival of Etoile Bakery, as was the strong sense of purpose that Holly had to continue to provide customers with some light relief from their own challenges through the pandemic. And staying positive is what carried Holly through the darkest hours. "Through it all, keeping a positive attitude was really important," Holly says. "Getting through the last few years and still coming out on top meant I had to be bold, confident, and look for opportunities even when it felt like there weren't any."

We often find this in businesses that endure tough times and successfully navigate them— they can often turn out for the better in the long run. The owners and employees are more confident in what the company can do and how it can pivot to meet the changing demands of the markets they serve. "If anything, I feel like I could have been bolder with some of my choices," Holly says. "If I weren't such a perfectionist about things, I likely would have opened the cake school earlier."

Spirits are still high as Etoile Bakery looks ahead to several more years of baking delicious cakes and confections for all of London. Holly is even thinking of expanding her creative ventures by finally giving attention to an aromatherapy business she had been thinking of for several years. When this business launches, and we know it will, we're certain Holly will apply what she learned with Etoile Bakery through the pandemic – staying positive, making bold choices, and embracing your confidence will get you anywhere.

"Just as one candle lights another and can light thousands of other candles, so one heart illuminates another heart and can illuminate thousands of other hearts"
— Leo Tolstoy

Chapter Seven

Keeping Mentally Moored While At Sea

As Seafarers kept the world economy moving through the increased challenge of lockdown, a network of missionaries went above and beyond to support them and their families as they transported essential goods to global ports.

IN A WAY, THE story of the Ever Given is the story of the pandemic. In March of 2021, the mega-size container ship Ever Given ran ashore, went sideways, and blocked the entire span of the Suez Canal for six days. For each of the six days, everyone watched the absurd moment unfold - even in the age of the pandemic where everything seemed surreal - the Ever Given was something many of us remember.

I watched this drama unfold from the comfort of my home on the TV while replying to emails on my laptop. Chances are, you did too. Like anyone, we all had challenges during the pandemic - schooling the kids at home, being separated from family members, connecting with loved ones over Zoom, and having an endless diet of takeaway and grocery deliveries. But we at least got to experience all of this at home, with our families.

Imagine having to deal with the anxiety of the pandemic while you were totally isolated away from your home, your loved ones, and even dry land. Not only did the crew of the Ever Given have to endure the drama from the ship's deck, but they also had likely been on that ship, non-stop, for close to a year. Meanwhile, commentators noted the implications of traffic through the Suez Canal coming to a standstill. Over 150 ships, accounting for nearly $10 billion in world trade, were in a holding pattern waiting to pass through the canal. Some were waiting for a week, others much longer, and every day they waited was a shockwave through the supply chain and the world's economy.

The previous year had already challenged the supply chain for everything from food to cars to microchips. Ships like the Ever Given waited for weeks at ports all over the world to unload their cargo so they could make the next shipment, and every day they waited was a day they weren't earning. Everything that happened at seaports around the world would eventually trickle down to your local stores, where common goods were out of stock for months. In total, more than 90% of the world's goods and fuels are transported on these ships from one country to the next, one continent to the next. Without them, the world economy would grind to a halt. It was quite an eye-opener for many people who had taken the global shipping industry for granted up to that point.

Critical to these ships are the crew who work on them. The seafarers. They are the backbone of the industry that supports the world economy, yet they are largely invisible. Every ship like the Ever Given is crewed by seafarers - people who spend most of their time working at sea. In fact, there are 2 million seafarers across the world. Seafaring is one of the most dangerous and difficult jobs in the world. Just about anything can go wrong while on a ship. From mechanical failures that leave ships drifting and stranded to extreme weather that can threaten the ship's integrity, the risk for injury is everywhere on a ship. Piracy is a very real concern, as is desertion and ship abandonment. Owners will suddenly decide the ship is too much of a liability to upkeep, and they will abandon a ship, the crew, and the cargo without any means of support, payment, or even a mailing address to forward complaints to.

Seafaring is as mentally draining as it is physical. Enduring the elements, sleepless nights from time zone changes, the unique isolation that comes with not knowing foreign languages, and being away from your family for months on end while still going to sleep in the same bunk every night - it all tests the extent of what the human soul can bear.

It's not something most people think about, but it is what Mark Lawson-Jones has been focused on for years - providing spiritual support to seafarers all over the world in any way he can. For over five years, Mark has worked with the Mission to Seafarers ministry to provide mental, emotional, and spiritual guidance to anyone of any faith or nationality. I have been involved with Mission to Seafarers since my days of working in the shipping industry. I witnessed the great work they do for seafarers all over the world. In an age where a plane ticket or a seat on the high-speed rail can place anyone in another country in a matter of hours, seafarers can spend months at sea. And this was before the pandemic complicated everything. Suddenly some seafarers were spending over 18 months away from home and could not go ashore.

The Mission to Seafarers would meet with crews as they arrived at ports worldwide to lend a hand and be a friendly face. "A lot of our work is done in a confidential setting, so a lot of what we do isn't exactly publicised. Every day, thousands of seafarers trust us and use our services. To report what we do publicly could jeopardise the care and support we deliver to seafarers and their families."

Their mission became exponentially more difficult after the pandemic forced ports and ships to tighten their protocols to prevent the spread of COVID-19. Just as the Diamond Princess leisure cruise liner had to quarantine several hundred passengers for weeks after arriving at their final port, the crew of cargo ships was also required to stay on board. Even after months on the water, seeing nothing but ocean to the horizon in every direction, crews were not allowed to take desperately needed shore leave. A 'run ashore' to get medicines, essential supplies, or even just to take a walk on solid ground was now impossible. Seafarers are regularly separated from their families for months at a time. Their partners and children might be in The Philippines, Ukraine, India, or anywhere else in the world, and it is rare to visit their home port on a shipping expedition. More often, they are passing through ports halfway across the world.

In a matter of weeks, the Mission to Seafarer's mission of supporting seafarers became more important than ever, even as it became increasingly difficult to do what needed to be done. A huge part of what the Mission did was provide human, face-to-face contact with someone who expected nothing of them. Giving seafarers a chance to speak outside of a chain of command in a language familiar to them was essential to getting them to open up about their deepest anxieties. Mark remembered the increase in one-on-one talks with families of seafarers who were worried about the welfare of their seafarers. Another spike in one-on-ones happened right at the outset of the Ukrainian war. Anxieties hit differently when they are presented against the backdrop of global tragedies.

Mark knew their mission was more critical than ever - not just to help keep the global shipping industry afloat but also to preserve the lives and souls of the humans on board the ships. Not only did Mark and the Mission to Seafarers need to find their own light in these dark days, but it was also imperative they keep their own light on for others to find their way through trying times. Without shore leave, days on a ship feel like Groundhog Day. Day in, day out, the same routines that need doing to keep the ship moving and the crew safe - and to do all of this without the ready support of your family. Working in these conditions stretched seafarers' mental fortitude to the limit. While the internet kept many people connected with their families, it was also something of a curse. As good as it was to hear your kids' voices or to see your loved ones' faces on a video call, it was also how the news of the world reached the seafarers. They were still learning about friends and family who had passed on, children who were born in their absence, the persistent issues with money and maintaining relationships - all things they had to deal with remotely, leaving them feeling like they couldn't do much at all.

The stress was huge. Suicide risk increased immensely. But this was the challenge The Mission to Seafarers is equipped to support - chaplains like Mark are trained to intervene in suicidal situations. But with the lockdown, The Mission to Seafarers couldn't visit the ships and the seafarers couldn't come ashore. The people on the ships asked for all kinds of things, from modems to medical supplies, to get them through the pandemic. These were key workers, essential people to the world economy, and they had a tough time getting what they needed.

The team had to adapt. The restrictions of the pandemic meant they couldn't provide the same services, but they could still support seafarers. The Mission would order delivery for meals to the entire ship, fulfil orders at the supermarket, and deliver whatever goods seafarers may have needed. Onboard visits were replaced by "gangway visits" - meeting crews at the top or bottom of the ramps to the vessels to provide spiritual and emotional support, often having to yell over the wind, through a mask, or under inclement conditions.

The masks made these interactions difficult. The ship visitors had to learn entirely new ways to communicate. Not only were they adopting oral languages like Filipino, Russian, and Ukrainian, but they also had to adopt non-verbal communication styles. They say you can see an entire world of emotion through someone's eyes, and Mark had to learn what eye contact and body language meant from cultures all over the world. Russians composed themselves differently from Filipinos, and seafarers had a different way of presenting themselves compared to the typical land-bound person. The Mission to Seafarers visited up to a hundred ships a month, in a dozen different ports, and several ships in one day, and often numerous trips to one ship.

Meanwhile, the team had to look out for each other. Helping hundreds of people deal with their own emotional situations often meant you needed to field your own concerns to others. They would meet in car parks to share cups of coffee, talk about their experiences, and provide support. During these meetings, they decompressed and related stories of the day. Helping each other to stay positive in challenging times. It was a surreal experience; despite the challenges, sadness, and tears, there was also a lot of laughter, and colleagues became very close.

Through all of this, the team had their personal challenges to deal with. Mark himself fell very ill. During the pandemic he found himself in the hospital - a terrifying thought as medical centres worldwide were overwhelmed with COVID-19 patients in their ICUs. In his case, he lost a third of his body weight and developed two forms of cancer. One Monday saw Mark in the hospital for preparation for cancer surgery at nine in the morning and he was awake at three that afternoon after the procedure. The next day he was recovering at home but was walking four miles a day by the end of the week. With only a slight relapse, Mark was back with the Mission online in a fortnight; after four weeks, he was visiting ships. A month after the surgery, he was back to his usual running routines, even though he had been left with a chronic condition.

He pushed hard because he knew the seafarers needed him; the Mission needed him.

The times may have been dark, but Mark learned where the light shines the brightest. He had immense support from his family while he was in the hospital. While he knew hundreds of people through his years of heading parishes around Wales, the challenge of the pandemic brought his truest friends to the forefront. Mark had to address his own mortality, but this also meant he was discovering his meaning in life and during the pandemic: to serve others. Of course, there were tears and frustrations with his family and with the seafarers he served, but they still managed to share a lot of laughs. He shared incredible stories with people who had seen the world and had a lot of insights to share.

The ordeals strengthened his faith and his resolve. His marriage is stronger than ever, and he has discovered some of the closest relationships of his entire life. While he is still active with the Mission, he keeps an eye on his condition with frequent blood testing and scans. Meanwhile, he is still supporting seafarers. While it may feel like the pandemic is over for most of us, it is far from finished for those who keep the world moving. Many countries still have their ports on lockdown. Major shipping hubs are backlogged with logistical challenges. Seafarers are still sailing the seven seas, ensuring the world's economy keeps moving forward.

Amazingly, the number of visits to ships and the number of seafarers that the Mission spoke to during the pandemic was as high as before the lockdowns and restrictions. They could maintain their life-saving service just when it was needed most.

There are many lessons from Mark's experiences, such as adaptability and resilience, but the most important is the power of purpose and mission. This enabled him to stay positive in the darkest times, including his personal challenges. Even through the darkest periods, this sustained Mark and the Mission to Seafarers to continue to serve the seafarers in their time of need. Mark and the Mission to Seafarers are still there to support them every step of the way.

"Even the darkest night will end and the sun will rise."
— Victor Hugo

Chapter Eight

Late Night Lessons Of Key And Co.

The business adviser, trapped in his home office, unable to work closely with clients and colleagues, achieving record results while supporting businesses with strategic advice, coaching, and leadership support through the pandemic.

In 2019 I left my last job on the executive team of a private equity portfolio company in the shipping industry. Although I was ready to leave at the time, my departure was sudden and I didn't have a plan B. So following my departure, in the words of British politician Norman Tebbit, I "got on my bike and looked for work." I got out there and tried facilitating as many face-to-face opportunities as possible. I met loads of people from the network I wove together in the years of my career in Consulting and Industry. One thing led to another – I would be out having a meal with a connection, and we would start talking about their business. The more we talked, the more we started to identify their business problems, challenges, and opportunities. They brought up advisory roles and consulting projects that I might take on. CEOs were asking for my advice, and before too long, I was working on my first project.

It really seemed to happen quite by accident.

Then word got out. My approach proved extremely effective and addressed many of the common complaints clients have of conventional consulting firms. One project led to another and another. Before long, I was building out a consulting and advisory network and a client book. On the other end, I was tapping into my extensive network and using an innovative resourcing model to assemble diverse teams of experienced people to enhance the consulting work. I didn't employ anyone, and I only worked with independent industry-sector experts and independent consultants to deliver projects. Beyond that, I did whatever I could to get into the same room with clients. Face to face, eye to eye. I wanted clients to see me and know me so they could trust me. Gradually, I took on clients in the infrastructure, transportation, and energy sectors. And I soon found that my approach also worked in Financial Services, Consumer Products and other industries. Clients loved working with me because I offered what they couldn't get from a traditional firm. I had fresh ideas, a practical approach, an agile network, and the appetite to help them to achieve amazing results. Key & Co. was born.

And clients loved it, so I kept at it. I had found my plan B, and it was only a matter of time before it turned into my plan A.

LATE NIGHT LESSONS OF KEY AND CO.

Buoyed by 2019 being a good first year for Key & Co., I was hopeful that 2020 would be the year of 10X growth. I went into the year with a fresh rebrand. I was wholly invested in building and developing new relationships and setting higher standards than ever - both in the clients I worked with and the projects I delivered for them. This was contingent on getting in front of and talking to as many people as possible about my unique offering.

Then, overnight, I was trapped in my home office. No one was going anywhere, but more importantly, I couldn't go anywhere. It felt like the lockdown took my playbook for the year and threw it out the window. At the start of the pandemic, many people thought this was a matter of a three-week lockdown. Three weeks turned into three months, and it wasn't hard to figure out that we would be in this for the long haul. I was extremely concerned that consulting as we knew it was now impossible. Game over. What would I do? Should I retrain and do something else? If so, what? My clients seemed to be in the same boat. They were totally disarrayed and under extreme stress at the sudden changes in conditions. Who would take on a consultant with all that uncertainty while their bottom line was compromised?

By the next morning, the panic had left my system, and I started to see the opportunity in the madness. This was a new circumstance with new variables, which meant we had a new playground full of endless learning opportunities. My clients still had challenges, and I was perfectly placed to help them. But we had to adapt quickly to the new environment. I quickly organised weekly calls with colleagues to start and maintain a conversation about what we were learning in these unprecedented times. What worked? What didn't? What turned out to be easier or harder than we expected? I even collected the greatest hits of these conversations in my book: *Late Night Lessons From The COVID-19 Crisis*. The pandemic had shown that business fundamentals hadn't changed, and things like leadership, purpose and planning were more important than ever. These were all precisely the things that Key & Co. could help with.

I kept serving my clients, but remotely. While I still appreciated being in the same room as them, I also realised that my experience of living and working all over the world made the location irrelevant. I could be anywhere, they could be anywhere, and a webcam with a Zoom or Teams link meant we could be together. Through these calls, the Key & Co. team advised our clients about the best moves they could make to keep their business going through the pandemic. I reassured them that they had what it took to keep things moving upward and to the right, manage the crisis, and motivate their teams. Even though I wasn't in a physical room, I was still winning new clients and delivering products with the same reliability and effectiveness as ever before.

I may have been working from my home office, but I rarely felt like I was truly "trapped" in there. The world kept moving and things kept happening. Who in the UK can forget the daily, nonchalant briefings from Boris Johnson? Or the time when he was almost killed by the virus! Or the "eat out to help out" programs to keep local eateries in business and the excess of gluttonous calories we consumed while home working? Or the daily exercise we did to maintain the gluttonous calories, our mental health, or even just to give our arms and legs something to do. No one was organising or hosting marathons, so I ran my own marathon in my garden. There were some off moments, too. For one, Christmas was more or less cancelled in 2020 in the UK. The day came and went, but the festivities and services didn't.

But through all of this, my business grew with clients needing our support. On top of it all, juggling remote learning for our four children was an added challenge – or a special kind of torture? Our clients had similar, and worse, to deal with, with the deaths of family and friends, in some cases, separation from loved ones. The pandemic was all-encompassing and it was happening to all of us. Its effects were close to home. Friends and family were struck by the virus, and people I knew passed away. The shopkeeper at the end of our road died. The virus affected everyone. Personally, professionally, or otherwise, this proved to be a challenging time for everyone.

In business, the time was difficult, but only if you wanted to look at it that way. In reality, it might have been the best thing to happen for many businesses out there. It took us from a mindset of "this is the way things are done" to "we can do this any way we want to." And not just for myself and Key & Co., but for my clients and colleagues – many of whom are featured in this very book. After enduring the pandemic together, I am closer than ever to many of my clients. We developed more effective ways to work together. Key & Co. has more clients, more consultants, and more repeat business since the pandemic began. Today, I'm proud to claim a wide and diverse client book that features an impressive international network of clients.

Taking time to reflect on these successes, I'm reminded of the lessons I learned in my late-night calls. Like our clients, Key & Co. thrived through the pandemic thanks to our strong sense of purpose: to serve our clients and help them through the global challenges they faced. We demonstrated leadership of the joint Key & Co. and client teams to address challenges and realise opportunities. We doubled down on good planning and resource management and invested in building and motivating our teams, safeguarding them, and ensuring their wellbeing. We innovated, adopted new technology, and pivoted with great agility, always focusing on our clients. Above all, we remained positive. Our mindset and attitude each day was: what can we do today to help our clients get through this? And we transferred this to our clients, helping them to see the light in the darkness.

The very word pandemic often brings a sense of panic and dread. It implies a lack of control and outcomes we could never imagine. But in this case, the pandemic delivered hugely valuable lessons and opportunities for Key & Co. and our clients. Thanks to the circumstances we faced, we are now clear on what we need to do to continue serving our clients, to grow, and to survive and thrive when the next crisis comes around. Many are now turning their attention to the next challenge as the climate crisis looms. What will this mean for their business and its markets? How will they decarbonise their own operations? How can they support their customers in achieving their net zero commitments? How can they change their business models, products and infrastructure? We are pointing them to the lessons we learned through the pandemic and helping them translate these to the next challenge.

"There are flavours in it, insinuating and remote, from mountain torrents and the scanty soil on moorland rocks and slanting, rare sun-shafts."
— Aeneas MacDonald, 'Whisky'

Chapter Nine

The Angel's Share from the Devil's Cut

A sustainable whisky distillery that weathered the crisis, keeping the team safe, and building a new and novel brand that takes the market by storm, transforming the whisky industry forever.

T HE LAST THING YOU may think when it comes to whisky is "new." From the amber colour of the liquid to the glassware, labelling, folklore, and branding that showcase the varieties we have all come to know, whisky is very much thought of as an "old world" kind of spirit. Once it is distilled, it must be aged at least three years in barrels – and if you are waiting to realise profits from your whisky, those three years can feel like a lot longer. Just think of the first three weeks of lockdown that we all endured – even that felt like ages!

For an established whisky brand, the pandemic might not have had a significant impact on how they ran their business. When your product just gets better with age, you only benefit from letting it sit in the storehouse for another year or two while you sell other inventory to keep afloat. Unless, that is, you're new to the market and need to make a name for yourself. Even more so, how could you establish your new brand in an age when no one was out and about for an evening of fun and revelry? Can a new alcoholic drinks brand launch without the pubs, bars, and restaurants being open?

That's the question Annabel Thomas reckoned with as the launch of her company, Nc'nean, was derailed by the pandemic. Not only because of the disrupted supply chains and opportunities for distribution and discovery, but because Thomas was attempting to make whisky sustainably – something unheard of in the industry.

Annabel attended the University of Cambridge and then went to work for Bain & Company, a global consulting firm. While at Bain, Annabel worked on secondment for Innocent Drinks, a UK company producing a variety of fruit juices, seltzers, and other products. Although the start of her career might suggest a different story, distilling was written in the stars for Annabel. Her grandmother was part Scottish and her parents had bought a farm in the Highlands Whisky region. In 2009, her father had the idea of building a distillery on the farm. With some irony, it should be noted that her father was a chairman of DrinkAware at the time. Also, at this point Annabel hated whisky.

Yet, a single-page business plan was born from the idea. And, like all good business plans, a huge amount of research went into it. Thomas discovered that no one in the industry talked about sustainability when it came to whisky production. Her time at Innocent showed her the value of having a purpose-led business – Innocent is known for their natural ingredients, and sustainable sourcing and production practices – but there was no equivalent among whisky brands. Furthermore, most distilleries are owned by giant beverage conglomerates. These companies are huge, even if the brands under them seem independent. Consider Diageo, which owns Tanqueray, Lagavulin, and the Johnnie Walker line. Suntory, which owns numerous Japanese whisky brands and even Jim Beam and Maker's mark. And let us not forget Pernod, which owns Jameson, Absolut, and the Glenlivet brands. All of these are multi-billion-dollar, global brands who have had their knee on the neck of the spirits market for decades.

What would it take for a newcomer to break in? Especially when you want to take a sustainable approach to a typically conservative, traditional, and stodgy industry like whisky distilling? It turns out, it would take a lot of help from unexpected places. Knowing she may never get another opportunity to do something so unique, Annabel split her time between consulting, Innocent drinks, and what would become Nc'nean, and got to work raising money, collecting investors, and working with master distillers, engineers, and contractors to get the Nc'nean facility up and running. They broke ground on the build in 2015 and, as one might expect, things moved slower than they would have liked. The remote location of the farm meant limited labour was readily available. Furthermore, it was a more technical build than the contractors were used to as the stills would be powered by a biomass boiler – a key component to their sustainability effort.

2017 came around and the aging process started. To be officially labelled "whisky," the product must age for three years. The widespread practice is to routinely distil and age the product in a cycle – barrels are emptied and bottled at various ages through the three years. The longer the spirit stays in the barrel, the more flavour and colour it gains. Barrels are refilled with fresh spirits and the process starts anew. After the first of the alcohol went into the barrels, the company went to work establishing their brand – there was no time like the present to start getting the world excited about what was coming!

Speaking of exciting things that were on the way, Annabel welcomed her daughter – Mimi – right about this time. All the while, she was traveling between London and the distillery, spending a week here and a week there to oversee operations. Nc'nean had run for seven years with minimal revenue through some tours and sales of botanical spirits, and Annabel was ready to make all of that change – the team was preparing to open for business with a huge launch ... in the summer of 2020.

Yes, like every one of us, Annabel was hobbled by the global shutdown caused by the Pandemic. However, there was a blanket exception for those who worked in food and drink. It was essential for people to eat! But it also begged the question: how essential was whisky? While I'm certain there are those among us who could make the claim that a steady supply of alcohol was essential to how they managed their day to day during lockdown, Annabel was faced with the question: how would she keep the distillery running, and was it morally right to do so? Worldwide, people were falling ill, dying, and facing dire economic straights - and here was Nc'nean, creating what many would consider a non-essential, luxury item.

Above all, Annabel wanted to keep her team safe, which partly meant they had gainful employment and something to focus on while the world struggled through the lockdown. There was very little risk of COVID infiltrating the village or the peninsula where the distillery was located – the challenge of the remote location of the family farm ended up keeping her distillers safe. But Annabel wanted to maintain a good reputation in the community – both in the village, among the employees, and with the distillers, servers, and drinkers who would soon enjoy her product. This meant keeping a small, isolated team on site to continue working while having the rest of the company maintain their distance. This meant a lot of time online, through Teams and Zoom, to address problems and create solutions. While those who lived North were used to having limited contact with others, Annabel noticed it was the younger staff – those who lived in the city and were used to working in offices and gathering in pubs – who were most affected by working from home.

Add a child to the mix, and Annabel was more eager than ever to keep things moving and launch the brand to the world. Most people expected a three-week shutdown before things would get back to normal, but then the next two years dragged on. In the whisky business, taking even a six-month hiatus can have monumental impact on sales and production. On top of it all, there were no on-trade sales happening. In the alcoholic drinks world, new customers and brand recognition happens in the pubs, bars and restaurants. The company had hired an on-trade salesperson who would, ideally, visit pubs, bars, restaurants, trade shows, and other industry-centric places to sell their stock. The shutdown meant no pubs or bars, which meant no on-trade sales, which meant Nc'nean had to find another way to get word of their product out there.

The one thing that didn't shut down during the pandemic? The internet. Annabel and her team amplified their online presence by hosting an auction of the first ten bottles of their whisky. Still caught up on the moral question of "how can we encourage people to spend money on our drink when the world is struggling?", proceeds from the auction would go to a selection of five charities, a local trust, two organisations focused on sustainability and two supporting the hospitality industries.

Leading up to the auction, Annabel visited the distillery to watch the first ten bottles come off the line and took those ten to the auction house. In all, Annabel thought they might fetch about £20,000 for their efforts.

To their amazement, the first bottle went for £41,000!

By the end of the auction, they had raised £92,000 – averaging about £18,000 to each of the charities. Annabel was blown away by the results of the auction and the demand kept growing as the pandemic went on. The £41,000 bottle put them well on the map for whisky lovers – a community who avidly buys special editions to resell and trade online. Their online presence exploded and delivered a wealth of visitors to their website and social media pages.

The on-trade salesperson was now exclusively off-trade – focusing their time on getting the whisky into bottle shops and liquor stores for retail. The focus was simple: get the product to as many small, independent retailers as possible. The demand for Nc'nean was high, and this demand would surely turn into additional traffic for the small businesses. The distillery couldn't get the next batches bottled and shipped fast enough.

Why did Nc'nean's strategy work so well?

Diageo, their largest competitor (and the largest liquor brand portfolio in the UK) realised little opportunity from their ecommerce platforms. Historically, and through the pandemic, Diageo relied on the established relationships with Tesco and Sainsburys to move their product and keep it top of customer's mind. For the brands that survived with on-trade sales – such as Gordon's Gin – things went south, quickly. It's hard to be the top-selling well-liquor when there isn't anyone to order from the well. Focusing on digital marketing was as important as it was new. The Nc'nean team would turn on the camera to host cocktail making tutorials, virtual tours of the distillery, and at-home tastings so they could offer the rich experience of discovering a new product no matter where their customer happened to be. For better or worse, at-home drinking was on the rise – so why not make it classy?

Also: Facebook ads. The return on their investment into Meta's advertising platform was huge. "It was like getting a license to print money," Annabel remembers. She was new to Facebook ads and figured it was the "normal" way to do business. In a way, she almost felt guilty at how easy it was to sell the whisky online. It was another pandemic phenomena. Since then, expectations about online advertising have been adjusted considerably. Post-pandemic, post-shutdown, the Facebook advertising machine isn't quite as prolific as it was when everyone was stuck at home.

Above all, Annabel and the Nc'nean team had the unwavering support of their investors. They stayed on and offered support even when the pandemic darkened prospects all around the world. Although, it's not that they could have pulled out – all their money was tied up in capital! Biomass boilers aren't exactly something you can easily liquidate – not that they would have needed to. In fact, Annabel remembers that they even took on new investors right before the shutdown took place – but even they took it in stride.

"Of course, we learned a lot through it all," Annabel tells me much later. "No matter what business you're in, you have to be prepared for the unexpected." For one, "global pandemic" is now on the distillery's risk register. Also, the flexibility of communication through Teams proved so effective that it is still their primary means of keeping everyone up to date now the pandemic is over.

"Making money is hard. Really hard!" Annabel notes. And it's true, if you have ever attempted any sort of product-based business, you quickly find out that making sales and turning profits is challenging.

There are always hidden, unexpected costs and you end up wishing the margins on your product could be just a little bit wider. But they persisted. Of all things, the COVID-19 pandemic steeled her resolve to her values. She had set out to create the best whisky in the most sustainable way possible – even if that meant it was rarely created with the most cost-effective means.

The biomass boiler, which had been the mainstay and logistical headache of their operation, didn't make sense from a profit and loss perspective. Every boil left a dent in their ROI, but it was always the right thing to do, the sustainable way to distil the alcohol. In fact, post-pandemic, as the Ukrainian War taxed energy resources throughout Europe, the economics of the biomass boiler ultimately became an advantage. The boiler became even more central to the ethos of the operation. These values went all the way down to the ingredients that went into the still. Local, organically grown barley is never cheap – especially when it is purchased at production scale. Yet, it was the right thing to do to support the local economy and reduce the carbon footprint of the whisky. Also – it makes for a far superior product. And, again, when the Russia-Ukraine conflict flared up, the economics of locally sourced grain became an advantage.

(Author's note: trust me, you can taste the difference in the final product.)

"Everything they tell you about business, all the stuff that seems like a given, you gain a crystal-clear understanding of how essential it all is once a challenge like the pandemic comes along," Annabel says. "All the way down to taking the time to recruit and hire people who are a good match for your team – we wanted people who had the enthusiasm for the product and the drive to grow their role." Matt – the on-trade sales rep. hired before the pandemic – rolled up his sleeves to learn about the trade beyond the sales process. With the master distillers he learned about blending flavours from the barrel. He made mean cocktails and shared stories with visitors about what made Nc'nean so important.

Hiring the right people is critical. During the pandemic or at any time. Annabel learned this, and was thankful for it, early on. The pandemic kept her out of the distillery and away from the people who were making the product – but she trusted them to put in their best work because she had taken the time to find the right people. Having the right team also means you can be more flexible when challenges come up. Before the pandemic, Annabel might have kept a 4+ year marketing plan on the books – not unlike what the major whisky brands do. Bucking tradition, she now has a quarterly plan that might change quickly and is much more agile. "When it came to the distillery and production, I learned to listen to my gut instead of waiting for someone to tell me what the right answer is," Annabel says. "As long as the team is happy and the risk is low, go for it."

In the years since, Annabel and her team are continuing to shake up the world of distilling. Nc'nean is now a certified B-Corp distillery – one of only two Whisky distillers in Scotland with the title at the time of writing. This was mainly taken on by Amy, the visitor manager, in the days when on-site tours were minimal, and time was plenty. B-Corp is not an easy thing to attain but the efforts are well rewarded by audiences everywhere. Between Annabel (now a reformed whisky-hater), Amy, and the rest of the Nc'nean team, the focus remains on bringing diversity to the whisky industry while creating the best product through the most sustainable means. In a male-dominated industry, in a pandemic-stricken time, Nc'nean tells a story of surefooted perseverance.

Annabel also changed the way whisky is enjoyed. It's no longer a libation for old men in tweed jackets. Nc'nean honed their marketing to appeal to both men and women and younger crowds. By simply adding soda to create a long drink at the bar, the appeal of whisky notably widened into bars and restaurants throughout the UK. Plus, younger crowds love the idea of something that is produced sustainably! Often, it may be the deciding factor when selecting a product off the shelf.

"We know we have the right people behind us," Annabel notes, "Just take a look at our followers on Instagram. Our Whisky really is a drink for everyone.

By that metric, I'd say they are doing just fine.

Cheers!

"Live with passion. Stop living someone else's dream and pursue what you're passionate about. When you do, you will beam with passion."
— Eliud Kipchoge

Chapter Ten

Keeping on Running

An athletics club that kept training through the pandemic, its members keeping safe and staying physically and mentally fit, smashing personal bests while adapting to the situation.

O NE FOOT IN FRONT of the other, and the other, and the other. Again. And again. Breathe in, breathe out. In through the nose, out through the mouth. Mind your pace, this isn't a sprint and we will get to wherever we're going in due time. This is running. This is the one thing I know I can do because so many people do it. It can happen any time. For most of us, we aren't running for any other purpose than to get back to the front door we started from.

This is running.

For many of us this is our salvation. This may as well be a lifesaver.

As I compiled information, interviews, and research for this book I connected with many clients and friends about their perspective of how the pandemic changed them, their business, and their communities. I found that there were common themes in business that also showed up in organisations and sports teams. And these same themes resonated with my own experiences of getting through the pandemic.

Since 2015 I have been an active participant with the Herne Hill Harriers, an athletic club here in London that coaches and trains track and field athletes of all disciplines. When I joined, I had just run the London Marathon and found myself wanting to take my stride further. While I may not have Olympic ambitions, I wanted my next marathon to be more than a tour through the city and to realise my full potential.

If you are involved in athletics in the UK or have watched the London Marathon, you may recognise the Herne Hill Harriers (from here on, HHH) by their red-and-blacked hooped vests. Founded in 1889 and currently training at the Tooting Bec Track in South West London, HHH is one of the most successful and inclusive athletic clubs in the region. Members range from under under 11 years to 90+ and include Olympians, former and current among their number.

HHH has endured world wars, changes in governments, monarchies, and more. The world will always change, but people's drive to move, compete, and improve is always persistent. Within the club there are a number of training groups and the one I run with in particular comprises more than 40 male and female athletes.

The group is overseen by Geoff Jerwood and Keith Newton. Both are lifelong athletes and have committed decades of their lives to running, training, and coaching. At their peak they produced national and international level times in cross country and road running events, including the marathon. They established our training group in 2011 as a sharp, fast training group with a structured training set-up, meeting several times a week to train and racing over multiple distances and surfaces throughout the year. Geoff and Keith are more than just the coach you might see standing on the sidelines with a stopwatch in hand, both are heavily involved in registering, coaching, fundraising, and the other unseen, unsung logistics of the club. Indeed, both Keith and Geoff have been president of the club. Like every good coach, they are the support system for their athletes – celebrating their victories and guiding them through the losses. Keith and Geoff prepare tough training sessions for their athletes, and a place for them to train – which recently meant working to secure over £500K from the Wandsworth Council to resurface the track. These coaches are dedicated to the sport, and this dedication is what led the group through some tough years. As we know, there have been quite a few losses and sacrifices in the last handful of years. As the world started to shut down to contain the spread of the COVID-19 outbreak, every single person was asked to assess every aspect of their day-to-day life. Did you still have a job? An income? A place to live? How did your kids get to school? Where did your next meal or food shop come from? Most of all: how much of your day was now idle because you no longer had a commute or a social schedule to keep?

Like any other organisation at the turn of the year, HHH had no inkling of the scale of the pandemic to come. They wanted 2020 to be a year of growth. New memberships, new training programs, a bigger presence in more races throughout the area. They wanted to continue diversifying their membership to include athletes from every discipline and background. However, like any other organisation in 2020, those plans were all put on hold as the world went into lockdown. The pace came to a halt, no one knew what they were or weren't allowed to do, and the routine that so many people had relied upon and built their days around was no more.

This meant races and competitions were cancelled. Some events were postponed indefinitely, some running clubs disbanded permanently. But HHH got over the shock of the lockdown and quickly started putting in practical solutions for the growing problems. How could we keep people moving?

If there was one race they weren't interested in placing second, it was the race against COVID. But running against COVID felt like racing on a continuously changing course. We had no idea what we were permitted to do. At one point there was to be no group running at all. But a few weeks later it was deemed okay to run in pairs, and then in groups of up to six. Then, a month later we were locked back down again. It was tricky and some running clubs didn't bother keeping up with the changing situation; staying shut down was easier than keeping pace with what was required.

Through it all, Geoff and Keith did everything they could to keep the club and the training group together and keep their athletes on track with their training. Not surprisingly, many of the strength and conditioning sessions were outlined and shared through Facebook. On WhatsApp, the group chat was lively with jokes, stories, updates, and other banter from across the group. When we were allowed, we arranged to meet up and run in pairs (or groups of 4, 6, or whatever was allowed at the time). Geoff's emails to the group meant everyone stayed connected and kept on running through every phase of the crisis around us.

Technology was essential to keeping the groups together training and racing. We ran 5km and 10km races virtually. Even the 2020 London Marathon was a virtual event. The marathon was without spectators and only open to qualified athletes who passed a COVID-19 test. For everyone else, you could submit your times for running a marathon distance. The registration fee was donated to charity, which ended up securing the Guinness World Record for being one of the largest single fundraising events in the world. Fitness apps like Strava opened up running to entirely new audiences to track and share their runs with other users and across social media. You could even create "Strava Art" by plotting a course that would create a line drawing. Intricate pictures of animals, faces, and landmarks were created.

Running, it seemed, was having its moment. And while the world was struggling with a devastating virus, most of us were taking up healthier habits. Beyond HHH and other running clubs and athletic organisations, UK citizens seemed to excel at prioritising exercise. A daily walk, a weekly run, or even at home yoga and strength training. According to *Run, Repeat*, the average runner increased their exercise levels by 117% during the pandemic. In May 2020, just a few months into the pandemic shutdown, Nuffield Health reported that 76% of British people took up at least one new form of exercise after the lockdown started. Scottish Athletics reported a rise in membership at 50 different clubs. All over Britain, new run clubs and fitness groups sprung up. And why wouldn't it? People wanted a reason to move and to be together – no matter how socially distant they needed to be.

As for HHH, they worked to keep their athletes progressing and training while staying within the social distancing regulations. Geoff and Keith were careful to make sure they were giving the right advice. Whatever they could do to keep the club moving and growing, the club did it. Subscription fees were waived, online seminars and training sessions were held, and there were plenty of opportunities for the club members to keep training.

As a result, rather than back off the training, runners got fitter and faster and smashed their records. Personal bests were achieved at the highest rate in the history of the sport. As for the throwers of javelins, hammers, and discus – these were much more challenging. It was hard to practice in the park when the track was closed! For everyone else, the running was a lifesaver. As the world changed around us and the situation and daily news was depressing, a long-distance run was the core, consistent part of our day. It kept our physical and mental health in check, even if it was just a reason to go outside. For those with mental health challenges, many of which were exacerbated during the lockdown, clubs like HHH were an opportunity to connect with other people while benefiting from the consistency of regular training. Running was a lifesaver. For many, it was what got us through the pandemic.

Today, now that we are on the other side of the worst of the pandemic and the lockdowns, the HHH ethos continues. Of all things, the lockdowns helped the club focus on its mission and deliver a better experience. The club is still dedicated to offering track and field opportunities to everyone aged under 11 to 90+. Today, the outdoor training groups are larger than ever – with more than 40 runners training together on run nights. HHH has celebrated success with their national cross-country team and supported Olympians – including Katie Snowden from the group – who competed at the Olympics in Tokyo and routinely represents England in competitions all over the world.

With every sport, with every race, a coach designs the training block so the athlete faces more resistance. Resistance is what builds strength and endurance, and what provides a suitable allegory for everyone coming out of the pandemic. Anyone who lived through the experience isn't likely to forget the handful of years the world was thrown into upheaval. We all had opportunities to learn and to do something in a completely new way – what we did with these opportunities determined how we persevered.

HHH had over a century of experience and perseverance by the time the pandemic hit. The organisation had survived other global events, and they were certain to make it out of the COVID-19 outbreak. This time around, the establishment of communicative technology – from livestreams to tracking apps to a jovial WhatsApp group – only served to further what the club had set out to do. There are many more races to run, and the members of HHH are more conditioned than ever to succeed in them.

"When you're sad, you're not sad. You are merely oblivious to the good things in your life. There is always a crack of light in the darkness. Find it."

— Dianna Agron

Chapter Eleven

Out of our Depth: An Endurance Swimmer's Lessons

The endurance swimmer, drawing on her inner strength to navigate the pandemic, and pivoting her speaking business to an online model, with lessons for us all for another pandemic and other challenges.

August 9, 2019. Anna Wardley lowers herself down the cold metal ladder. It's 11 at night, at least eight hours before first light, and 20 miles to the east is her destination: the Californian Peninsula dotted with millionaires settling into sleep in their seaside estates that are bought and sold for their priceless views. Adrenaline burns through her every limb as her legs sink into the inky black waters of the Pacific Ocean. She has trained for this. She doesn't know how long it will take or what challenges she will face en route. She'll just swim in the vast, horizonless darkness until she gets there.

Anna loves a challenge, especially when it comes to long distance swimming. Seven months before the world went into the unprecedented lockdown to curb the spread of Covid-19, she swam the Catalina Channel between Santa Catalina Island and Long Beach, California. The iconic stretch of water off the coast of Southern California is one of the world's classic channel crossings and it had been in Anna's sights for several years. Naturally, the year she trained to swim Catalina coincided with more sightings of great white sharks than ever before. But for a long distance sea swimmer, that was all part of the challenge.

I know Anna through the Clipper Round the World Yacht Race. We were crew members on *Hong Kong Clipper*, sailing through high seas on a 68-foot yacht. This is where I first came to witness Anna's determination and resilience as we experienced the toughest sailing conditions, thousands of miles from land. As in the Covid-19 pandemic, these were conditions where people's inner strength and determination were revealed.

Little did she know that the particular challenge of crossing the Catalina Channel would pale in comparison to what we, collectively, would face in the coming years. A test of strength, grit, endurance, and compassion. In 2013 Anna became the fourth person to complete a 103-km non-stop, solo swim around the Isle of Wight off the south coast of England. That feat took 26 hours and 33 minutes to complete. The sea was relentless. Sometime in the middle of the night she was swimming against the tide and was swept back two miles in a single hour. When daylight broke, the tide turned in her favour and pushed her towards the finish. None of this happens without focused training and dedication, and she would soon discover that the endurance you gain while training for a particular sport often supports you elsewhere in life.

Anna started late at night from Catalina because she wanted to avoid the strong afternoon winds the area was famous for. Following the international marathon swimming rules, she wore her regular swimsuit, cap, and goggles. Wetsuits aren't permitted as they would provide extra buoyancy and protection from the cold. Lights were attached to the goggles – red on the left for port, green on the right for starboard – to help Anna's support team keep tabs on her while she swam alongside the support boat.

All the while, she tries not to think about how this boat has a passing resemblance to the vessel featured in the film *Jaws*. In addition to her support team, there are two independent observers on the boat – each tasked with ensuring all of the rules are followed so her swim qualifies. This means no-one is allowed to touch Anna in any way and she can't make any contact with the support boat or kayak. Every half hour, food and water is passed to her by a telescopic net to avoid any accidental contact.

Painkillers are also allowed and she takes regular doses pushed into the top of peeled bananas. Between the bone-chilling water and the night air, plus the exhaustion that tens of thousands of swim strokes puts on her shoulders, everything about her body hurts. Everything tells her to stop.

Not that she has anyone to tell this to. For Anna it is just her and the ocean, hour-after-hour of monotonous swimming through the darkness as the cold pushes her to the edge of her consciousness. With just a word, it could all be over. Her crew could pull her into the boat and cover her in warm, dry blankets and bring her to shore within an hour. Instead, she digs into her reserves that come from a deep well of childhood adversity. Some would call this resilience - a hackneyed word she tends to avoid using, but it's possibly the right one in this context.

She tells herself: whatever she does, she cannot get out of the water. It's off the menu. It's not an option. No matter what mental turmoil she finds herself in, no matter what kind of compromise she tries to make with herself. She is not getting out of the water. This is the resilience, this is the endurance, this is what she has learned about herself through tackling some of the world's toughest swims: she can withstand adversity and she is hellbent on making it to the other side, whatever it takes.

Just like her circumnavigation of the Isle of Wight, she finds herself in a strong counter-current as she gets closer to the Californian coast. She shouts at the waves, *'I'm going bloody backwards!'* She punctuates her statement by punching the water in frustration – she knows this is futile, but sometimes that's all you can do.

18 hours and 31 minutes later she crawls up a beach under a huge star-spangled banner flying high on the cliffs above her, unable to walk after so many hours of continuous swimming. The flag is posted at the Trump National Golf Club Los Angeles. Maybe the President was wrapping up a round of golf at his club that afternoon, looking over to see a worn-out swimmer crawling up the pebbles to clear the surf. More likely, his Secret Service detail would have spotted her first. All of them, all of us, would have had no idea as to the challenges the next year would bring.

But unlike him, Anna's experience in the Catalina Channel would reinforce her capacity for endurance that would enable her to embrace the periods of isolation that Covid-19 would bring us in just a few months.

In 2019 Anna was awarded a Churchill Fellowship that gave her the opportunity to travel to the USA, Australia, and Scandinavia to research how to improve the support children receive after a parent dies by suicide. Anna lost her father to suicide as a child – one of the many challenges that fed her resilience later in life – and her mission was to improve the support for other children left behind after suicide. Towards the end of that travel in March 2020, Anna had to fly back to the UK from Denmark with just a few hours' notice. Denmark announced they were closing their borders that night. The world started to react to the pandemic.

No-one in the UK will forget the address Boris Johnson, then Prime Minister of Britain, would give to the nation on 23 March 2020. This was the announcement that everyone, as a country, must stay at home for at least the next three weeks. People could only leave their homes under special circumstances: to buy essential supplies or medication, to care for a vulnerable person, to exercise outdoors or to go to work, but only if it was not possible to work from home.

On one hand, there was a sense of relief that the British government finally introduced definitive measures to control the spread of the virus, especially after crowds of people gathered at parks and beaches the previous weekend to soak up the long-awaited spring sunshine after a miserable, wet winter. It seemed that self-interest had won over collective responsibility, fuelled by confused messaging over what people should be doing in the face of this new virus. Johnson had to act. Infections were rising relentlessly and the National Health Service faced overwhelm. A few days after the televised address and the start of lockdown, data released by Public Health England revealed that the UK had 11,658 confirmed cases, a rise of 2,129 cases in just 24 hours. Deaths had risen to 578 from 475, the first increase of over 100 in a day.

It was made clear that the three week lockdown was the best-case scenario. The measures introduced could well be extended. We were all swimming in uncharted territory and trying to adjust to a new reality. How long would we be cooped up and separated from one another? How widely would the infection spread? Anna had additional reason to worry: she was pregnant with her first child after a long IVF journey.

What tips did Anna have as an endurance swimmer for coping with life in lockdown?

Firstly, don't become overwhelmed by the magnitude of what lies ahead. There is little use in thinking about the weeks and months to come. Just focus on how you are going to organise yourself today and for the rest of the week. When swimming, Anna never allows herself to think about the entire distance she needs to cover. If she did, she'd be paralysed by the enormity of it and would struggle to ever leave the dock.

Instead, she focuses on swimming to the next feed, and then to the feed after that, until she eventually reaches the end. She doesn't wear a watch and her support crew are briefed not to tell her how far there is left to go. All that matters is that she swims until she gets there. With the Covid-19 lockdown, we had no idea how long the freedom-restricting measures would be in place. But from her experience in the water Anna knew that, one day at a time, we'd get there.

Secondly, use your energy only on the factors you can control. Anna can't control the ocean or the weather, but she can control her mindset in the moment and how she prepares for a swim. During lockdown, you can't control the fact that you're confined to your home, but you can control what you do with your time whilst you're there. Organise your time, set a routine, and take one day at a time.

Thirdly, stay positive. Your mindset determines how you cope and it's one of the few things you have control over. Reframe the confinement as an opportunity to reconnect with family, sort out the loft, or pick up a mothballed creative project. Whilst swimming, Anna makes mental lists of what she is grateful for to keep fear and self-doubt at bay. Negative thoughts can quickly spiral and impact your overall wellbeing. Steer clear of scrolling news and social media, as this only tends to fuel fear and worry.

***

Still, we watched as intensive care units were overwhelmed with the infected, who were stripped of human contact and hope. So many of us were worried about how the pandemic would impact our personal economics. Anna was self-employed and expecting her first child. The lockdown wiped out her bookings and income overnight. Her work as an open-water swim coach and keynote speaker was stocking the reserves for her maternity period. Suddenly, it was gone and she was left in a precarious financial position. None of us knew when the restrictions would be lifted, but there was one thing on the calendar that Anna knew couldn't be cancelled or postponed in those extraordinary times: the arrival of her baby.

Earlier on, a week before we went into lockdown, the UK government's Chief Medical Adviser, Chris Whitty, announced that pregnant women were deemed vulnerable to the virus. This meant Anna needed to avoid all non-essential contact for at least 12 weeks. This advice was quickly compounded by new restrictions on movement and social contact that applied to everybody. Anna was to spend the remainder of her pregnancy alone and confined to her home.

Thankfully, Anna's baby seemed oblivious to all the mayhem that was unfolding outside of the womb. In this time, she focused on a routine of exercise and connecting with others on the phone and online. Every morning, without fail, she joined a group of people all round the world to dance together on a video call. It got her moving, and brought some joy and connection in the strangest of times. It may have also given her daughter, who experienced the movements from inside, an early and innate love of dancing.

Anna spent hours walking along the beach with her ageing dog, Deefa. The fresh air and connection to the sea was important to her even when swimming was prohibited. Watching the tide come in and out helped her reflect on the impermanence of every challenge that we face. As with any tough swim, she knew the tide would turn. What pushes you out will eventually bring you in.

Anna saw her midwife and together they listened to a strong heartbeat. It was a moment of pure magic, especially given the backdrop of a world in lockdown. The maternity unit was scoured clean and the only other mum-to-be in the waiting room arrived wearing two pairs of latex gloves. With a fabric headband covering her mouth and nose, Anna tried to offer her some kind of reassurance through eye contact, but all she could see was fear in her eyes. She looked back at her phone for the latest news updates, seeing if she could work out what sort of world her baby would be born into as she waited to be called in for the ultrasound scan.

As her pregnancy progressed, Anna developed complications and had to attend hospital several times a week for scans. For each visit she arrived with a bag packed, ready for a potential admission and delivery. In any circumstances this would be challenging for a first-time mum, but even more so when attending all the appointments alone and in full personal protection equipment.

Anna also did a lot of writing, both for publication and for herself, to help process what was happening and how she was responding to it. She wrote for her unborn child to record the extraordinary times that they would be born into. In the months after giving birth, she contributed to the anthology *Born in Lockdown*, written by women who became mums for the first time during the pandemic. Her daughter will dig it out of her memory box one day and read it in disbelief.

Anna also used this time to focus on finishing her report for the Churchill Fellowship. As travel restrictions remained in place, she conducted the final interviews on video calls. She wanted to make sure everything for this fellowship was completed before her child arrived.

She continued to focus on what she could control instead of dwelling on everything that she could not. Having lost all her in-person bookings, she switched to speaking online, sharing her insight as a long-distance swimmer into coping with adversity and challenges with audiences around the world.

One of the first virtual engagements involved delivering the annual Resilience Lecture for members of the British Armed Forces who logged in from their various bases around the world. It was only when addressing them that Anna realised just how much resilience she'd needed to cope with the situation she'd faced in those early days of the pandemic, with fear of what lay ahead for both herself and her unborn baby.

We learn the most about ourselves and each other in the toughest of times. Almost five years on, the intense fear and existential threat to our very survival has faded, but the scars remain. The best tribute we can pay to those who lost their lives in the pandemic is to focus on what there is to learn from our collective experience. To reflect on what light could be found in the darkness.

For Anna, the light arrived early in August 2020, four months into lockdown, when her daughter was born in the midst of one of the hottest days on record. The thermometer hit 39 degrees right as the hospital's air conditioning went out of commission. But no amount of discomfort could quell the joy she felt that day. All of these months, all of these challenges, all to overcome the odds and bring a new life, new hope, into the world in the middle of a global pandemic.

Anna published her Churchill Fellowship report entitled *Time to Count* in December 2021 and founded Luna Foundation three months later as a means to implement her key recommendations. She didn't want her report to gather dust while sitting on bookshelves so she created Luna to ensure that children who experience the death of a parent through suicide get the support they need and deserve. Anna's mission is to help them to find light in the darkness and instil a sense of hope for the future.

From her pursuit of the Churchill Fellowship, which gave rise to the Luna Foundation, to the creation of new life during a global lockdown, Anna's story epitomises the era's theme: finding light in the darkest of times.

"**H**OPE IS BEING ABLE to see that there is light despite all of the darkness."
— Desmond Tutu

Chapter Twelve

A New Chapter And Long COVID

The rower, whose Olympic dream was thwarted by the pandemic and who is now raising awareness of the long COVID pandemic that continues to affect millions of people.

A LTHOUGH YEARS MAY HAVE passed since COVID-19 first dominated headlines and the pandemic long declared "over" and "normalcy" resumed, there is still a considerable population who struggle with the impacts of the virus. The day to day routines and economics of life resumed, but for some the effects of the pandemic linger on with those who have Long COVID. On the surface, Long COVID sounds like what you think it would be: the symptoms of COVID last for a longer period of time. A majority of infected patients were back on their feet within a week or two, but for Long COVID sufferers the ailment can drag on for months and years.

Furthermore, the symptoms of long COVID are more diverse and continue to baffle doctors and scientists as they start to develop treatments. For some patients, Long COVID can show up time and again as relapses of varying severity and returning the patient's progress back to zero. As of this writing, an estimated 1.9 million UK residents are suffering from Long COVID. The symptoms are varied - from respiratory and digestive distress to mental fog and overall fatigue - and the available treatments are still in the early stages.

Still, 1.9 million in the UK and upwards of another 400 million people worldwide have had the condition at some point since the beginning of the pandemic. Some economists estimate Long COVID strains the world economy to the tune of $1 trillion pounds a year. And while my assessments of the COVID-19 pandemic may be tied to local businesses and economies, I always want to bring the focus back to the individuals who endured the experience - and Long COVID is no different. In the case of Oonagh Cousins, the COVID-19 pandemic derailed her Olympic debut, but Long COVID continues to be a significant deciding factor in her day to day life and her long term ambitions. I met Oonagh through one of our annual Key & Co networking events where we were raising awareness about Long COVID and I, and the other guests, listened to her recount her fascinating story.

Rowing is a part of the Cousins family tradition. Oonagh followed in her mother's footsteps by joining the rowing club at Gonville and Caius College at University of Cambridge - something her mother had done a generation before. For Oonagh, rowing was a hobby - a way to exercise and meet people - until she witnessed the Boat Race in 2015. The energy, excitement, and passion around the rowers and the race ignited her imagination and fuelled her desire to row. After a year learning to row at college, she joined her university's rowing team where her height and strength stood out among her fellow athletes. She thrived while training alongside the former Olympians who were training in the squad. She could hold her own on the rowing machines next to championship rowers even though she was still relatively new to the sport. In 2016 she served as an alternate for the University Boat Race Squad and in 2017 competed in the reserve race. Every race was an opportunity to learn and grow.

During her final year at Cambridge, Oonagh tried out for U23 and was ultimately selected to race for the team in the summer after she graduated. It was this selection that helped her solidify her decision to pursue a career in rowing, ultimately wanting to make the Great Britain senior team. If she managed to secure a spot on the senior team, she would be able to train full time at the national training centre in Caversham and compete for a spot on the World Championship and Olympic teams.

To get here, she moved to the University of London Boat Club where her efforts would earn her a spot on the Great Britain senior team in early 2019. By March 2020 she was pre-selected to join the team that would compete in the Olympics later that year., while her selection should have been cause for celebration, a dark cloud hung over that day. By this point, the pandemic was prominent in the headlines and was a growing concern around the world. Immediately after the announcement, coaches closed training facilities and instructed the team to train at home. A few days later, the 2020 Olympics were officially postponed in an effort to prevent the spread of COVID-19. The coach put the entire team, including those who had earned a seat on the boat, back on reserve. The coach would reassess the situation in the coming months and allow team members to re-earn their spots.

By then, Oonagh had developed a persistent, nagging cough. Yes, she came down with COVID-19. Like so many others, she was stuck at home, on the couch, with the energy to do very little over the coming weeks. She knew her body and what it would need to quickly recover (fluids and food to fuel the recovery!). While other members of the team had also contracted COVID-19, their recovery seemed to be far faster than Oonagh's, letting them return to their training regiments. But for Oonagh, the cough led to debilitating fatigue and insomnia, brain fog and confusion, (and what she now knows was dysautonomia and MCAS?). Remember, in early 2020 the virus was still anybody's guess - prevention, treatment, and symptom management were still unclear. While medical organizations and governments raced to find solutions, Oonagh struggled to recuperate.

Any attempt by Oonagh to resume her training was immediately thwarted by her debilitating symptoms. After months of this, Oonagh and the team doctor, Ann Redgrave, made the difficult decision: Oonagh would not be ready for the postponed Tokyo Olympics. It was devastating news.

And this was only the beginning of the journey with the illness. The timeline for a "return to normal" or effective COVID-19 treatments was completely uncertain. Vaccines were still months away, and no doctor could offer a clear prognosis. There were no reliable treatments, and the condition's symptoms and duration were wildly inconsistent. The virus didn't discriminate—it affected people with underlying health conditions and those in peak physical condition, including Olympic-level athletes. Doctors could only advise her to rest and hope her body would recover. Some reassured her she'd be back to normal in a few weeks, but those weeks turned into months.

Drawing on her years of physical training, understanding of her body and the limited knowledge available about Long COVID, Oonagh adopted a strategy of "aggressive resting." This is exactly what you think it is: a priority on rest, sleep, and nutrition. And it seemed to work. In October 2020 she was still only able to do 4-5 hours of basic tasks (showering, cooking, short walks) in a day. But over the course of that year, she made steady progress, with her daily capacity slowly increasing. By September 2021, Oonagh felt close to recovery. The second dose of the vaccine gave her what felt like the final 5% of recovery . She was able to resume her training, she wanted to get back to sport.

She started with three small sessions a week and gradually increased to 12 sessions per week. She joined ULBC and competed in the Henley Royal Regatta in the summer of 2022.

After a year of training and a summer of racing, she felt ready to re-join the GB Rowing Team. However, the increased training volume that came with returning to the team triggered a resurgence of her symptoms. Looking back, she now recognizes that she should have heeded the warning signs and stopped, but driven by her determination to return to her former life as an athlete, she pushed herself to keep going. Her body started sending clear signals—persistent ear, skin, and eye infections, along with a developing knee injury. It wasn't until a conversation with her former coach that she began to understand what was happening and understood the need to rest. Once she finally stopped, the adrenaline that had been keeping her going drained away, and the full force of the relapse hit.

The news of Long COVID side-lining an Olympic athlete caught the media's attention, as it challenged the narrative that COVID-19 only affected the elderly and vulnerable. Oonagh first appeared in the BBC Sport in October 2020, and then continued to appear in various media outlets (Sky Sports, CNN, ITV, Radio Five Live) throughout the pandemic.

It also attracted people with questionable intentions. In November 2020, Oonagh was contacted by people who claimed they had a process that would teach her to rewire her brain and improve her Long COVID symptoms. The pandemic, as with most disasters, are a breeding ground for fraud and exploitation - and this program was no different.

"They were trying to suggest that I could think my way out of the symptoms, and I disputed it entirely," Oonagh told BBC. She was horrified that such programs were being marketed to those already struggling with illness, suggesting their symptoms were psychological. The potential harm caused by such messaging was deeply concerning. Even more troubling was the exploitation of vulnerable individuals—people desperate for recovery and willing to spend money in hopes of improvement. While Oonagh knew that Long COVID and other post-viral illnesses were poorly understood and lacked adequate support, this was her first encounter with the narrative that these conditions were somehow fabricated. Given the profound impact Long COVID had on her life, she was outraged that such harmful ideas were being perpetuated. She discovered her experience was far from unique. Historically, when an illness doesn't have a test or concrete parameters for diagnosis, the public tends to brush it off as something the sufferer is imagining - "if you can't treat it with a pill, then it can't be real."

When Oonagh first became sick she knew there were few treatments available for her condition and wasn't surprised that doctors didn't know how to help her. However, her experience with the brain retraining program showed her the challenges the patient community faced in just being taken seriously. She felt that given she had a platform as a professional athlete to speak out she should try to use it to raise awareness of the debilitating impacts of the illness, and its very real physical causes.

A NEW CHAPTER AND LONG COVID

After retiring from professional sport, Oonagh continued her advocacy work and now is working in the Long COVID space. Her first role post-rowing was as an Engagement Fellow at the University of Oxford, where she worked on a social science research project using participatory research methods to explore tools to help individuals with Long COVID communicate their experiences. Since September 2024, she has worked as a Fundraising and Communications Associate at Long COVID Support, a UK charity dedicated to advocating for and supporting individuals living with Long COVID. In this role, she is focused on supporting the charity's growth and impact. . Oonagh is also involved in the #ThereForME campaign, which advocates for political action on post-acute infection syndromes (PAIS), calling for accelerated biomedical research and improved NHS care for those affected by these conditions.

Through this experience, both of being chronically sick and being forced to abandon her rowing career, Oonagh feels her perspective and values became stronger and more defined. Whether it was from her rowing training regiment or during her period of "aggressive rest," a few things remain central to her experience. She offered a few of these points:

- **Growth Mindset:** Focusing on continuous improvement instead of the need to prove oneself. Embrace learning opportunities and cultivate curiosity.

- **Process over Outcome:** Ensure you are getting value from the journey, not just the end goal. The outcome is probably out of your control at least to some degree (you might get Long COVID and not be able to compete at the Olympics), but if you're committed to learning and growing through the process, even if things don't go as planned, you'll likely find yourself in a positive place in the end. The process itself holds its own rewards, regardless of the result.

- **Achievements, no matter how significant, are transient**—once they pass, the next challenge awaits. Many Olympic medallists, for example, struggle with their mental health after winning. They might have believed the medal would bring lasting happiness only to find that it doesn't. We often place too much emphasis on big achievements while forgetting that our happiness is shaped more by what we do each day. The way we spend our days is the way we spend our lives, so ensure you're content with how you're living day-to-day rather than fixating solely on the outcome.

- **Wellbeing:** Recognize the mind-body connection. Prioritize sleep, nutrition, and hydration for both physical and emotional health. Losing my health changed who I was—things that once brought me joy no longer did, I withdrew from social interactions, and even the simplest tasks became overwhelming. My ability to process information, think clearly, or write properly were severely compromised. While Long COVID is a more extreme example of compromised health, wellbeing exists on a spectrum. Even without a diagnosed condition your wellbeing is a core part of who you are. If you're constantly run down, not getting enough sleep, or not eating well then your thoughts, emotions, and interactions with others will be impacted in a negative way, limiting your ability to live the life you want and be the person you aspire to be.

- **Emotional Awareness:** During the years of being long term sick to attempting a return to rowing, followed by a relapse, the emotions I faced were overwhelming. It would have been easy to avoid or suppress them, but I chose to confront them head-on, with self-compassion and reflection. I asked myself questions about what emotions I was experiencing and why, which lead to questions about who I was beyond rowing, what I truly valued, and how I could move forward in a way that was meaningful to me. It wasn't a quick process, but by sitting with the grief, I came to terms with the fact that life doesn't always go as planned. I found peace with the experience. I believe until we take the active steps to process the difficult emotions that come with difficult experiences, those emotions will linger and continue to influence us and have a hold on us. While there will always be a part of me that feels the loss (that represents how much rowing and that part of my life meant to me), I'm now living a life I'm really grateful for and proud of—one that wouldn't have been possible if I'd stayed on the path I had envisioned before Long COVID. Processing my emotions allowed me to truly move forward, without letting the weight of the past continue to shape my future.

- **Connection:** When it all felt hopeless and I wasn't sure if I'd ever be "normal" again. It was the support of my loved ones who listened and gave me comfort in my darkest moments that kept me going. My family and friends gave me the strength to endure a little longer. Genuine human connection provides an incredible source of resilience when facing life's challenges. In my work, I hope to offer that same strength to others. Embrace empathy and the power of human connection—it's one of the most important things we can give and receive.

Oonagh's journey, though marked by setbacks and unexpected detours, ultimately reveals a resilience forged through the fires of adversity. While the Olympics may have slipped from her grasp, she has found herself as an entirely different kind of champion.. While the headlines throughout the pandemic focused on the global economic and social impacts, the real newsmakers were the individuals who were finding their way through the darkness. Oonagh's story is a testament to the human spirit and a reminder that even in the face of immense obstacles, there is always the potential for growth, connection, and a renewed sense of purpose.

"The past can hurt. But the way I see it, you can either run from it, or learn from it."
— Walt Disney

Weaving The Common Threads

F OR DECADES, VIROLOGISTS WORLDWIDE warned us of an imminent outbreak. For the most part, we rarely listened to them. Even as SARS, MERS, and Ebola made rounds through pockets of the world, we still didn't heed the warning. Even if you aren't a doctor or virologist, you always knew something catastrophic could happen. The entire course of human history is littered with massive disruptions from plagues and influenza. We know the power of the microbe, the essential need to wash our hands and prepare food correctly. We all know that touching an elevator button or walking through a crowded hallway can result in a head cold that could put us out for a week.

We know these things happen, but we never expect them to happen to us.

For years I had seen the phrase "Global Pandemic" on just about every risk register my clients published during my career. The possibility has always been in front of us, even if we could only imagine it through the Hollywood lens. We were repeatedly warned to prepare and stockpile supplies and prepare for an economic squeeze.

Everyone predicted the COVID-19 crisis, but no one expected it to happen. And when it did happen, we were all forced to react. Coming from a business mindset, it's always better to be proactive and prepared. The last global influenza pandemic of comparable scale was in the early 1900s – anyone who knew what it took to survive something like that has long since expired. How can you be prepared for something you have never experienced before?

This book contains just eight stories of the pandemic. But of course, you can find hundreds of millions of stories like these across the world. Every person, team, and business has their story and everyone is unique, but I outlined some of the common threads of these stories in my previous book, *Late Night Lessons From The COVID-19 Crisis*. These common threads include the necessity of having a strong purpose and vision, the importance of leadership, effective decision-making, innovation, collaboration and motivating a team. Everyone in this book, in some way, used technology to endure and thrive through the pandemic. For many, it completely changed how they conducted their business even after the most threatening days of the pandemic passed. But more than technology, we saw the importance of a positive attitude.

Something fundamental to human nature runs through this book: positivity and survival instinct. After lockdowns started and the world changed overnight, after we felt the shock of our "normal" life get pulled away from us, after we looked at the cards on the table it was those with a positive outlook who fared best. Even in the dark days of the lockdown, the best attitudes led to the kind of creative thinking and collaboration that turned into opportunities. The pandemic response showed that humans are inherently resilient and good at responding to immediate crises; we have an immediate and inherent survival instinct that kicks in. We saw that the most successful businesses and teams all had this in common. Even when things got difficult, they never gave up. They leant into the crisis rather than shying away. They found energy and motivation when they had to. They found light in the darkness.

"A ROOSTER CROWS ONLY when it sees the light. Put him in the dark and he'll never crow. I have seen the light and I'm crowing."

— Muhammad Ali

Reflections Three Years On

WE'RE NOW TWO YEARS out from the first edition of Finding Light in the Darkness, and three years since the end of the lockdowns, and as more time passes the less we seem to be learning. Yes, *less*. Even today there are still ways we can observe and quantify the impact from the pandemic years, but it doesn't feel like these learnings are going to make as big of an impact as they need to. In London in November 2024, more than a hundred million Tube journeys were recorded in a single month, according to Transport for London – numbers not seen since before the pandemic. The takeaway? The city's mayor, Sadiq Khan, has said these numbers show the region's economy is "roaring back." By some measure, this has always been what we have been striving for, hasn't it? The pandemic is over when the economy recovers, regardless of the rates of infection or deaths or stability of our public health systems.

There is a saying: never waste a crisis. The pandemic is now "over," and there is a risk that we waste an opportunity to learn from such a global, all-encompassing experience. Consciously or not, we were all so determined to get back to some kind of normalcy that we have largely failed to take away the truly important lessons of the COVID-19 crisis. Worse yet, we're are still facing numerous other major challenges – such as the threat of climate change – and the lessons of one crisis aren't being applied to the next.

Early on in the pandemic, just as the world was locking down and the economy went into turmoil, we quickly saw the huge economic and social disparities highlighted. Some were described in this book, and others were so common we almost didn't think about them. Many of us found ourselves working remotely from home, while having to also juggle all of the household chores and facilitate the education of our children. Many more still didn't have the option to work from home; either made redundant, forced to go on furlough or one of the "essential workers" in the healthcare, delivery, or food production lines of business. The pandemic split the world into those who ordered delivery, and those who did the delivery. According to Forbes, 500 people became billionaires during the pandemic. The wealth of the top richest people in the world doubled and the wealth of billionaires increased by 30 %. But did the increase in average wages of workers keep up with this added wealth, even though these were the people most vulnerable to the impacts of the pandemic? We all know the answer to that.

There were also the persistent challenges that came with people's general health. Deaths from COVID and its complications were staggering, but so were all the other fissures in our healthcare systems that came to light. How we took care of the elderly and immunocompromised or how the general public trusted the NHS and its workers was brought under harsh scrutiny. Today, at the end of 2024, there are tens of millions of people worldwide still suffering the wide-ranging symptoms of Long COVID – an issue that receives nowhere near the level of attention or seriousness that it should. Albeit, the list of symptoms – ranging from dizziness and brain fog to stomach pains and difficulty breathing – and the varying degree of their severity makes Long COVID a difficult disease to diagnose and treat. While it can be a truly debilitating disease, there is nowhere near the urgency or resources to studying it compared to the vaccine development during the pandemic.

Everyone wants to move on from the COVID years. In a way, we have, by just living out one day to the next. There is a desire to forget and to look forwards rather than backwards. But businesses are still recuperating, economic disparities are still rising, and people are still suffering from the losses. Meanwhile, the investigations into how the pandemic was handled can seem more about placing blame than they are about constructive reflection moving forward. The UK COVID enquiry is expected to cost more than £200M and many charities and victim support groups are deeply frustrated in its slow pace and – so far – lack of practical findings and recommendations. In my consulting and advisor work I'm always looking out for the lesson to be learned from any situation. Win or lose, there is always something that can be applied for next time. The success of your future may depend on what you learn from the here and now. The pandemic was probably the single biggest event to learn from that most of us have experienced in our lifetime and we must make sure that we all take lessons from it.

Although I am frustrated by the missed opportunity, I do accept that we have learned some things and that things have changed for the positive. The spread of technology was significant. People who never thought to set up a webcam and broadcast themselves – for a concert or a church sermon – are now doing so on a regular basis. Some companies rebuilt their organisation for a remote-first environment – implementing and upgrading technology and ultimately making their employees more productive. It also gave a lot of people a new perspective on the meaning of work and the value they both provided and received between them and their employer. The move to remote work also drove a lot of us to live more eco-mindedly. No commute meant not having to drive. As delivery applications were honed through the pandemic, there are fewer one-off trips to the shops for example.

Beyond work, just about everyone learned how essential social interactions were. They rediscovered the value of their friends and family and the need for face-to-face contact, third spaces, and group events. A lot of us even rediscovered what it meant to shop locally and use our local shops and businesses more – you might not know how important your local economy is until it almost vanishes.

At first, we all waited for things to "go back to normal." Then we were worried about what the "new normal" would look like. And now here we are, in the new normal, living as if it were any other day.

While we can look at the headlines and conclude the same things that changed, I've been looking internally at how my own business has changed in the past year. I also reached out to those who contributed to the first edition of this book to ask them the same. The findings were illuminating.

For my own reflection, I really did see things go "back to normal" to some extent for my consulting and advisory network. But I also see a different, hybrid model, that has evolved as a result of the pandemic that sees us combine face-to-face with online. And we are seeing that online interactions can supplement and add to face-to-face. We are continuing to work from home and serve international clients through all of the digital channels we've invested in. By moving a lot of the work into an online environment, we are seeing far more collaboration than we did before. Also, when you are able to meet with someone more frequently through a Teams or Zoom call, you get a better read on their physical and mental health, which allows you to understand them and meet their needs on an entirely new level.

I also feel like I'm taking things more in my stride. It takes more to phase me nowadays. I am less bothered by cancelled events, missed invoices, late flights, traffic, and so on. Maybe it's because I now plan ahead better, thinking more into the future and being less reactive. Maybe it's because I've seen how bad things can get in the pandemic, survived it just fine, and know that nothing is worth losing your cool over.

However, the limit to how much we have all really learned has irked me, especially as I reflect upon it today: we could do so much better. When you look at everything we collectively endured, all of the challenges we had to face and the ways we pulled through it, why aren't we doing more of that today? It feels like a majority of the world has slumped back into complacency. For all of the inventive solutions we came up with in a short amount of time, why are we not applying the same energy to resolving global conflicts or developing a more sustainable way of life? Why we not translating the lessons from the pandemic to addressing climate change?

It all feels like a wasted opportunity.

I emailed some of the contributors to this book, I wanted to see how they felt about all of this. How had they and their organisations changed? What was new for them? Now that there was some space between them and when the world went into lockdown, what do they remember the most? What things are they doing differently? What is the same as before.

Rob Baker, the rowing coach who kept the Cambridge team together and in peak form during the shutdown, got back to me. "We try to be more efficient with our time, always making sure we're adding value without taking anything for granted. This way, we can effectively train our athletes and they still have time to work on their degree programs." As a team, they have an invigorated approach to solving problems and overcoming challenges – their togetherness during the lockdown created the kind of bond where they can rely on one another for creative thinking. What else has changed? "The pandemic strengthened my resolve to be flexible and find better ways of working. Every issue that comes up is a chance to improve something. Seeing how we had a month to train for the 2021 race I can only wonder what other major changes we can make that will lead to our next win."

Elsewhere, while the pandemic truly challenged Vicar Kit with keeping his congregation together, things are still going well. He has a new appreciation for how essential the church is to his community and the surrounding area, and communities rely on communication. Today, he is still using Zoom for everything from prayer meetings and bible study to social coffee meetups and conversations about racial justice. The church also send out prayers, information, and event announcements through social channels and email.

Beyond the digital, Kit and the church have invested in their garden as a space to hold celebrations year-round. From holiday lights in December to an Easter Garden in spring, the entire neighbourhood loves seeing the lights and decorations of the festivities. As great as Kit is doing, he still sees the issues. "There are issues around mental health, cost of living, and homelessness that were brought right to the surface because of the pandemic. We came together to create solutions, but was it enough? No. During the pandemic we celebrated the bravery of NHS workers, but now they are going on strike to get fair pay. What lessons have we really learned?"

I am particularly intrigued by our friend Stuart Goldsmith, the aspiring stand-up comic who found himself without a stage once the lockdown hit. "I am a different person now!" he says. "The pandemic showed me that I can adapt to quickly changing circumstances, which showed me I can do anything I want over and above simply following my comedy dreams. I now approach my work from a much wider perspective and wonder how I can wield my passions to help people, rather than just feed my ego." This revelation has changed so much for Stuart. He takes online meetings even if the client is just five minutes away, it helps him stay focused on their needs and take better notes. He also has steered a lot of his energy to concerns of the climate crisis. "I've done a bit more comedy online, especially around the idea of sustainability, to deliver climate comedy sessions to larger teams."

Stuart is currently performing a show about the climate crisis. He is using his ability to connect with people to deliver an important message. "I think the moment when we looked up and saw a sky without planes a lot of us were motivated to take meaningful action against the climate crisis. The pandemic shook people loose of the idea of 'it'll never happen to me' when it comes to the future. Here is a crisis, and it's happening to you! Now more than ever is the chance for huge, heroic change to happen."

That's an idea I would love for everyone to take into the future – that huge, heroic change can happen, and it can start with any one of us. For months, the pandemic was the only thing in the news. It was worldwide, it was happening to you, to everyone, and there was no way to escape it. Maybe this is what drove so many people, especially those in this book, to invent new ways of doing everything in their lives. From how they ran their business to what they did for a living to how they approached their lives – the changes were huge; the results were heroic. Should it take a global pandemic, with an infection rate in the hundreds of millions and 7 million dead, to get people thinking so heroically?

Necessity is the mother of invention, but what is the cause of complacency?

Think back to the pandemic for a moment and then to your current situation. Ask yourself: are you comfortable? Should you be? What heroic change could you make today?

"The only thing we learn from history is we learn nothing from history."
— Friedrich Hegel

Lessons For Future Crises

THE EFFECTS OF COVID-19 were nothing short of disastrous. Millions dead, hundreds of millions infected, entire economies disrupted, and a world forever changed. It could only be worse if we neglect to learn from it. We must not forget all of the unique learning opportunities this event presented us with.

The point of this book is to consider some of the lessons that businesses, elite sports teams, charities and community leaders learned from the crisis so that they can be applied to other challenges. And while I pray there isn't another pandemic around the corner, the next challenge is on its way. It might be a small hiccup in your supply chain or it might be something much bigger that could rock your business to its very core.

The book is not, and cannot be, anything approaching a comprehensive account of the COVID-19 crisis. Instead, it is a series of observations from one group of people working with businesses throughout the crisis and documenting their thoughts and reflections. I hope you find it helpful and that it triggers some of your own reflections.

Positivity – finding light in the darkness – is a constant thread throughout the book and is the most important lesson for us. But positivity matters so long as it doesn't extend to naivety. It is insufficient on its own and can even be counter-productive unless it is accompanied by tangible action. Indeed, you could argue that it was positivity and optimism that allowed the pandemic to take off. The optimistic assumption is that tomorrow will be better than today, that the graphs will always go up and to the right, and that the worst-case scenario will never arrive. But then again, why list "Global Pandemic" on your risk register if you aren't going to prepare for it? This is perhaps the most important lesson that is relevant for other challenges and crises.

The lessons I have drawn from the pandemic also lead me to draw parallels with the greatest crisis that we now face, climate change. In this book I have highlighted the importance of purpose, leadership, decision-making, technology, planning, innovation, teamwork, coordination, mindset and - above all - positivity. It seems to me that all of these apply to climate change and that we now have an opportunity to apply the lessons from the pandemic to addressing this next great challenge.

Good luck and keep learning.

Jon Key,

Key and Co Ltd.

"It was the possibility of darkness that made the day seem so bright."
— Stephen King

Timeline

There were three lockdowns during 2020/2021 in the UK.

Spring 2020 lockdown ("lockdown 1"). On 23 March 2020 the whole of the UK was placed under lockdown measures. Schools were shut, non-essential shops were closed, and the population was asked to work from home where possible and only leave their houses for exercise and essentials. These measures started to ease in mid-May 2020.

Winter 2020 restrictions ("lockdown 2"). From 14 October 2020, England entered local restrictions by tiers, followed by a four-week lockdown from 5 November 2020. Wales entered a three-week firebreak on 23 October 2020, followed by alert level 4 restrictions. Scotland introduced protection levels on 2 December 2020. This period ended on 4 January 2020, after which Great Britain entered a nationwide lockdown.

Early-2021 lockdown ("lockdown 3"). From 5 January 2021, the UK government announced a further national lockdown for England. Similar rules applied for Scotland and Wales, particularly the message to "stay at home", meaning that adults in Great Britain were under a national lockdown at the start of the year in 2021.

Acknowledgments

With thanks to all in the Key and Co. network.

Especially to Holly, Arnaud, Stu, Henry, Christian, Lucinda, Kit, Rob, Quinten, Mark, Annabel, Geoff, Keith, Anna, Oonagh, Venetia, and all the clients, consultants, advisers and supporters of Key & Co.

And of course, thanks to my tolerant and supportive family! Ali, Edward, Eliza, Isy and Ned (and Coco). And Mum, Dad and my brother Tim.

Also, thanks to David and Henry for helping to turn the amazing stories into this book.

About the Author

I was born in 1974 in Cambridge, where I grew up with my parents, Carol and Bill, and my brother Tim. I am a "towny" and a "gowny," having studied engineering at Cambridge University.

After obtaining my master's degree, I stuck around Cambridge for a hugely informative post-graduate year where I studied design, manufacturing, and management by visiting hundreds of companies, small and large, both in the UK and worldwide. The experience gave me a curiosity for business, which has stayed with me ever since.

I have spent my career both as a consultant and in a series of executive roles with public and private companies, while also running my advisory business. I specialise in solving critical and complex challenges with CEOs and their leadership teams.

Over the years, I have developed an extensive network of clients, colleagues, and friends and bring them together into teams with the experience and expertise to solve the most challenging business problems.

Along the way, I have taught English in China, competed in a Cambridge-Oxford lightweight boat race, taken part in a round-the-world yacht race, and run in fourteen marathons. I have lived in Africa, Asia,

Australia, Europe, and South America and have been lucky to travel to many exciting places and meet some extraordinary people.

I draw my inspiration and energy from my hugely talented, and somewhat eclectic, global network. I am fortunate to have my family's support; my wife Ali, children, Edward, Isy, Eliza, Ned, and our dog, Coco. We all live together in London, one of the most exciting and diverse cities in the world.

I passionately believe in learning from life's experiences – my own, and the experiences of others. Like each of you, I have had my own share of ups and downs, and I look for lessons from every experience to find the lessons than can be applied to new and future situations.

Getting in Touch

I hope you have enjoyed reading this book. Please get in touch if you would like to learn more about our global network of consultants and advisors. We would also be delighted to hear your own lessons from the crisis.

www.keyandco.org

mailto: corporate@keyand.co

If you would like to donate money to The Mission To Seafarers, please do so:

https://www.missiontoseafarers.org/donate

If you would like to donate money to Long Covid Support, please do so:

https://www.longcovid.org/

Anna Wardley is a record-setting endurance swimmer, award-winning social entrepreneur and inspirational keynote speaker. She created Luna Foundation to develop better support for children who lose a parent to suicide. Anna motivates audiences worldwide to embrace resilience and lead purpose-driven lives.

https://www.annawardley.com

www.ingramcontent.com/pod-product-compliance
Lightning Source LLC
Chambersburg PA
CBHW031632210526

45464CB00004B/1857